THE BIBLICAL BASIS FOR PURGATORY

John Salza

To the Holy Souls in Purgatory:
"Requiem aeternam dona eis, Domine,
et lux perpetua luceat eis."

Saint Benedict Press, LLC
Charlotte, North Carolina

ISBN 978-1-935302-17-9

Cover design by Christopher J. Pelicano

Published in the United States by
Saint Benedict Press, LLC
P.O. Box 410487
Charlotte, NC 28241
www.saintbenedictpress.com

Printed and bound in the United States of America.

THE BIBLICAL
BASIS FOR
PURGATORY

TABLE OF CONTENTS

PREFACE

L AST year, I was driving to work one rainy and foggy week day morning. Traffic was moving along fairly well when, suddenly, cars began to stop. The stoppage was so abrupt that I had to brake quickly to avoid hitting the car in front of me. There was an accident up ahead.

And it wouldn't be the only accident that morning. As I stopped my car and glanced in the rear view mirror, I noticed the car directly behind me. It was going very fast. Too fast. Based on its speed and distance from my car, I knew that that car couldn't stop before hitting me. I was stuck. So I called out to God to protect us as I braced myself to be struck. And boom! That's what happened.

Fortunately, God answered my prayer and no one was injured. The driver got out of her car and ran over to my side window, apologizing profusely. She confessed that it was entirely her fault and asked me if I was hurt. She told me how guilty she felt and humbly begged for my forgiveness. Realizing that I had sustained no injuries, I assured her that I was fine. I also forgave her on the spot.

There was one minor problem, however. The impact dented the back bumper of my car. As we surveyed the damage caused by the accident, the driver quickly agreed to pay for the repairs. I asked for her driver's license and wrote down her contact information. Of course, if she'd refused to pay for the damage, I could have taken her to court and the judge would have ordered her to do so. Fortunately, this would be unnecessary. She paid for the repair and the issue completely resolved.

What does this story have to do with purgatory? Keep reading.

In this story, we see the following: Someone commits an offense, confesses her offense, and is forgiven. However, after she is forgiven, the damage caused by her actions remains. Furthermore, she feels guilty about her infraction and will think about the accident for some time to come. She may even have a new fear of driving a car in bad weather. She must also make satisfaction, as a matter of justice, for the damage she caused, while it is in her power to do so. If she doesn't, she will be handed over to the judge who will compel her to pay for the damage. In that case, because she refused to satisfy her obligations while she had the chance, the judge would also punish her (perhaps by giving her a fine or suspending her license).

It should not be difficult for Christians to see in this story an analogy to our spiritual lives. We commit a sin, confess our sins to God, and God forgives us. Yet, even after we are forgiven, the sin has ongoing effects. For ourselves, we feel shame and remorse of conscience. We feel small and weakened. Sometimes we may even feel more disposed to sin. We don't feel the same as we did before committing the sin. And we know that these feelings are manifestations of God's justice.

Regarding the effects on others, we may have injured someone's reputation through the sin of calumny. We may have harmed someone's financial condition through greed. We may have hurt those we love through selfishness. In each case we know we have altered the balance of equity between us and those we have offended. Most importantly, our sins and their effects impede our union with our Lord Jesus

Christ, who commands us to be perfect, as our heavenly Father is perfect.[1]

Although Jesus requires us to be perfect, most people—even those who die in God's favor—never reach this state of perfection prior to their death. They died loving and fearing God but did not overcome the imperfections of their fallen human natures. These imperfections often include attachments to created goods, inordinate desires for earthly pleasures, and small but habitual sins. They also include the satisfactions still owed to God, to restore the equality of justice for the many sins that they committed during their lives.

If, as Scripture says, "nothing unclean" shall enter heaven,[2] how can these imperfect souls ever enter into eternal paradise? If Scripture teaches that without "holiness" no one shall see the Lord,[3] how can these souls hope to behold the face of the all-perfect and holy God? The answer: purgatory. In purgatory, God purifies the soul of its imperfections through the fire of His divine justice. During this finite but painful process, the soul is purged of its evil inclinations and makes final satisfaction to God for its sins. After the purification is complete, God admits the soul into heaven where it enjoys the Beatific Vision for all eternity.

Before Jesus exhorted the crowd in His Sermon on the Mount to be perfect as the heavenly Father is perfect, He told them to make friends with their accusers while they were still able to do so. Jesus warned them that if they didn't, the Judge would put them into prison and they would not be released until they paid the last penny.[4] In this parable,

---

1. Cf. Mt 5:48.
2. Rev 21:27. Scripture verses are taken from the *Revised Standard Version—Catholic Edition*, or the *Douay-Rheims* if noted.
3. Heb 12:14.
4. Mt 5:25–26.

Jesus is warning His followers about the rigors of purgatory and the debt of sin. If in this life we fail to pay our spiritual debt to God, the debt for our sins, we will be detained by the Judge in the next life until we have made full satisfaction for it.

* * * * *

Purgatory is one of the most divisive doctrines between Catholics and Protestants. It is also one of the most misunderstood. That is because the doctrine covers the most theological territory. To believe in purgatory is to believe in the Catholic understanding of sin, redemption, grace, and judgment. This means that purgatory is a dogma of the Catholic faith.

Unfortunately, many Catholics don't believe in or understand purgatory. There are many reasons for this. Certainly, simple ignorance—of Scripture and of Church teaching—is one reason. Another reason is the influence of our culture, which ignores and even denies the reality of sin in our world. This error has even trickled into corners of Catholic education, where there has been a de-emphasis on God's justice and an over-emphasis on His mercy and benevolence. We see examples of this at many Catholic funerals, where a white-vested priest assures us that the deceased is in heaven, where we will all someday be reunited. We rarely hear about the reality of purgatory and the need to pray for these departed souls. This becomes a grave injustice to those deceased who are suffering in purgatory and need our prayers for their deliverance.

Although it may sometimes be ignored by those who are more comfortable preaching about God's mercy rather than His justice, the doctrine of purgatory is in fact one of the most merciful and consoling doctrines that Scripture teaches. God purifies us from our defects precisely because of His mercy. God refines His children in the fire of His love so that they can fully attain to the joys of heaven. God perfects us for our own benefit, not His. As they say, "no pain, no gain." Through the pain of purgatory, we gain the bliss of heaven. Without purgatory, not only would those of us with unfinished spiritual business be unable to enjoy heaven, we wouldn't make it there in the first place.

There are some, usually Protestants, who do not under-emphasize God's justice, and who are familiar with Scripture, but still have difficulty with the doctrine of purgatory. However, when you get right down to it, these are the same people who have difficulty with the plain meaning of Scripture in other areas too. If these people don't take Jesus literally when He says "this is my body"[5] or "whose sins you forgive are forgiven,"[6] they are unlikely to take Jesus literally when He says that God punishes and forgives sins in the afterlife.[7] If these people don't take Paul literally when he says God condemns us to hell for our wicked deeds,[8] they are unlikely to take Paul literally when he reveals that we must pass through fire after our death to be saved.[9] A Protestant's denial of purgatory is invariably based on his built-in presuppositions about how to interpret Scripture, and not on what Scripture actually says.

Certainly, Protestants raise many legitimate questions regarding purgatory. For example, if Jesus died for our sins, why does anyone have to go to purgatory? If Jesus took on the punishment for our sins on Calvary, why would God punish us further after we die? If Jesus paid the debt for our

---

5. Mt 26:26; Mk 14:22; Lk 22:19.
6. Jn 20:23.
7. Lk 12:47–48; Mt 12:32.
8. Rom 2:8; 2 Cor 11:15; Gal 5:19–21; 2 Thess 1:8–9; 1 Tim 1:9–10.
9. 1 Cor 3:15.

sins, why do we still owe a debt after our death? Doesn't the doctrine of purgatory take away from Jesus' saving death on the cross?

These are very good questions, and in this book I hope to provide the answers.

*   *   *   *   *

Unlike what some Protestants contend, purgatory is not a novel teaching concocted by the Catholic Church during the Middle Ages to scare the faithful into giving alms and doing penance. As we will see, the doctrine of purgatory is explicitly taught in Scripture. The doctrine of purgatory is also found in the writings of the early Church Fathers, from the very beginning of the Church. This means that purgatory is a revelation of Jesus Christ given to His apostles. Purgatory is part of the Deposit of Faith "which was once for all delivered to the saints."[10]

In fact, the Jews, who were first to receive "the oracles of God,"[11] believed in a state after death where sins could be forgiven. God revealed this truth to the Jews in both Scripture and the prophetical tradition. In addition to the many Old Testament verses revealing how God purifies His elect through trial by fire,[12] we see the common Jewish practice of praying for the dead in the actions of Judas Maccabeas, one of the greatest warriors in Jewish history:

> For if he were not expecting that those who had fallen would rise again, it would have been superfluous and foolish to pray for the dead ... Therefore

---

10. Jude 1:3.
11. Rom 3:2. Pre-Christian and post-Christian Jews (particularly Orthodox Jews), as well as Orthodox Christians, also believe in purgatory. Today, Orthodox Jews are often seen praying for the dead at the Wailing Wall in Jerusalem.
12. Prov 17:3; Dan 12:9–10; Wis 3:5–6; Sir 2:5.

he made atonement for the dead, that they might
be delivered from their sin.[13]

Interestingly, although most Protestants claim to deny the
doctrine of purgatory, they believe in the doctrine implicitly.
Protestants admit that Christians continue to sin until the
end of their lives. However, they also confess that we will no
longer be sinning in heaven. It necessarily follows, then, that
there must be a final purification between death and eternal
life. Whether the purification happens instantaneously or
not is not the issue. The issue is that there is some kind of
purification that moves us from a sinful state to a non-sinful
state, and this is what the Church calls purgatory. Moreover,
it follows that just as we can pray for someone's sanctification in this life, we can also pray for his sanctification in purgatory. Popular Protestant author C.S. Lewis in fact argued
that our souls demand purgatory.

Indeed, reason alone demands the existence of purgatory.
After all, it is probable that most God-fearing people die
with at least small sins on their souls, or with sinful inclinations that they never completely conquered. Since nothing
defiled can be in God's presence, it follows that these souls
cannot be admitted into heaven with those imperfections.
And yet these souls, so close to God, are not deserving of
eternal hell-fire, for such a punishment would not be proportionate to the offense. In short, many departed souls are
worthy neither of everlasting punishment nor immediate
happiness. Because God desires all men to be saved, reason, then, insists on a transitional state where good souls are
cleansed of their remaining imperfections so that they are
made fit for the bliss of heaven.

---

13. 2 Macc 12:44–45. All Christians held the book of Maccabees as inspired
Scripture until the Protestant revolt in the sixteenth century.

The human heart also demonstrates that there is a purgatory. Who doesn't remember his deceased loved ones in his prayers? I bet there aren't many—even among those who, like Protestants and even non-Christians, don't believe in purgatory. Why do these people remember the dead in their prayers? Because desiring the well-being and happiness of departed family and friends is an instinct of the human heart. If there were only heaven and hell, how could we explain this instinct? In heaven, hope is unnecessary and happiness a certainty; in hell, hope is lost and misery guaranteed. The blessed in heaven don't need our prayers, and the damned in hell can't use them.

*   *   *   *   *

This book has three goals: First, to explain the biblical basis for purgatory by examining the relevant Scriptural texts and the writings and interpretations of the Church Fathers. Second, to inspire us to live holy lives and avoid purgatory by the many means Christ has given to us through His Church. Third, to encourage us to pray for our brothers and sisters in purgatory so they may be delivered from their sufferings. Pursuing these goals with faith, hope and charity will be pleasing to God, and merit for us both satisfaction for our sins and greater glory in heaven.

> If the work which any man has built on the foundation survives, he will receive a reward. If any man's work is burned up, he will suffer loss, though he himself will be saved, but only as through fire.[14]

JOHN SALZA
Feast of Our Lady, Virgin and Queen
May 31, 2008, Anno Domini

---

14. 1 Cor 3:14–15.

PURGATORY
AN INTRODUCTION

What Purgatory Is

ABOUT heaven, Scripture says, "nothing unclean shall enter it, nor anyone who practices abomination or falsehood, but only those who are written in the Lamb's book of life." (Rev 21:27). The word for "unclean" (from the Greek, *koinon*) refers to a spiritual contamination that must be cleansed before we can enter into God's presence. Habakkuk also says, "Thou who art of purer eyes than to behold evil and canst not look on wrong." (1:13). Because God is "holy, holy, holy," He will allow nothing to enter His dwelling place with the slightest spot or blemish. (Cf. Rev 4:8).

The word "purgatory" comes from the Latin *purgare* which means to purge, purify, or make clean.[15] The Church teaches that it is a place or condition of temporal punishment for departed souls who are destined for heaven but not completely purified from sin. Through this purgative process, spiritual contamination is removed and soul is made wholly pleasing to God so it can live forever with Him in heaven.

---

15. The Greek transliterated word for "fire" is *puroo*, from which we get the word "purgatory."

The Church often refers to the souls in purgatory as the Holy Souls, the Poor Souls, or the Suffering Souls.

Purgatory is demanded by God's justice. When we sin, we incur before God the liability of guilt and the liability of punishment. God forgives the guilt of sin through His mercy, but punishes the sinner by His justice.[16] If God's justice demands that sin be punished, it follows that one who dies with contrition for his sins but before satisfying the full punishment for them will suffer the remaining punishment in the afterlife.

Protestants often point out that the word "purgatory" is not in the Bible. On this basis, they conclude that purgatory is a false doctrine. This approach exhibits the common fallacy among Protestants, that something must be explicit in the Bible for it to be true.[17] Yet the Bible never teaches such a thing. Instead, Scripture commands us to follow both the written and unwritten traditions that Christ and the apostles handed on to us through the Church.[18] Nevertheless, as we will see, not only is the doctrine of purgatory part of the unwritten apostolic tradition (which we will see in the chapter on the Fathers), it is also expressly taught in Scripture. Therefore, to believe in the Bible means we must also believe in purgatory.

Protestants also reject purgatory on the basis that Christ has made complete satisfaction for our sins. While this

---

16. Scripture refers to the liability of guilt (*reatus culpae*) in Ps 5:10; 18:23; 25:11; 32:5; 51:2, 7; 68:21; 109:7 and the liability of punishment (*reatus poena*) in Ps 59:5; 69:27; 89:32.

17. If the titles of all true doctrines had to be in Scripture, Protestants would have quite a problem. The titles "Trinity," "Incarnation" and even "Bible" are not found in the Bible, yet are believed by all Protestants. Also, many Protestant doctrines are not found in Scripture or Tradition, like "total depravity" and "believer's baptism," as well as such novel practices as "altar calls" and "women pastors."

18. 1 Cor 11:2; 2 Thess 2:15; 3:6.

sounds like a pious thing to believe, it's misleading.

It is true that the sacrifice of Jesus Christ was more than sufficient to atone for all punishment (temporal and eternal) due to sin. The Passion of Christ was a superabundant work of satisfaction for the sins of the whole world. Christ gave the Father more than was necessary to compensate for our sins. As the Apostle John says, "And he is the propitiation for our sins: and not for ours only, but also for those of the whole world."[19] Both Catholics and Protestants agree on this elementary point.

However, although Christ alone has made satisfaction for the eternal punishment for sin, He specifically requires us to participate in making satisfaction for the temporal punishments for our sin. Temporal punishments refer to the personal, social, ecclesial, and cosmic effects that our sins cause, which must be remedied by virtue of God's divine justice. We participate with Christ by enduring the trials and sufferings of this life, as well as through acts of penance.

This is why Paul says, "Now I rejoice in my sufferings for your sake, and in my flesh I complete what is lacking in Christ's afflictions for the sake of his body, that is, the church." (Col 1:24). If Christ made complete atonement for our sins, then how can Paul say that there is something "lacking" in His sufferings? There cannot be, insofar as the remission of the eternal punishment is concerned. Only a being with eternal power could atone for eternal punishment, and that is exactly what Christ did for us. It necessarily follows, then, that what is "lacking in Christ's afflictions" refers to the debt of temporal punishment that we must suffer, in justice, for our sins. According to Paul, we are able to "complete" or satisfy this punishment that God imposes when our own

---

19. 1 Jn 2:2 Douay-Rheims (DR).

sufferings are joined to those of Christ. As we will see, God requires this suffering because it restores the sinner to the equality of justice and allows the sinner to achieve the holiness that is required for heaven. (Cf. Heb 12:10).

Because making satisfaction for our debt of punishment is difficult, Scripture warns us to fear the consequences of forgiven sin: "Be not without fear about sin forgiven."[20] Of course, if there were no consequences to forgiven sin, there would be nothing to fear. If we do make sufficient satisfaction in this life for our many sins and die in a state of grace, we will go straight to heaven. However, if in this life we don't "complete" what is "lacking in Christ's afflictions" for our sins, we will do so in the next, which is purgatory. As Paul says regarding God's judgment, "It is a fearful thing to fall into the hands of the living God." (Heb 10:31).

The Church's Teaching on Purgatory

Before we analyze the scriptures, let's see what the Church says about purgatory. In the Catechism of the Catholic Church we read:

> All who die in God's grace and friendship, but still imperfectly purified, are indeed assured of their eternal salvation; but after death they undergo purification, so as to achieve the holiness necessary to enter the joy of heaven. The Church gives the name purgatory to this final purification of the elect, which is entirely different from the punishment of the damned. The Church formulated her

---

20. Ecclesiasticus 5:5 (DR).

doctrine of faith on purgatory especially at the Councils of Florence and Trent.[21]

Based on the teaching of Scripture and the Church Fathers, the Council of Florence (1439) defined purgatory as follows:

> It is likewise defined, that, if those truly penitent have departed in the love of God, before they have made satisfaction by worthy fruits of penance for sins of commission and omission, the souls of these are cleansed after death by purgatorial punishments . . .[22]

The Council of Trent (1563) declared:

> Since the Catholic Church, instructed by the Holy Spirit, in conformity with the sacred writings and the ancient tradition of the Fathers in sacred councils, and very recently in this ecumenical Synod, has taught that there is a purgatory, and that the souls detained there are assisted by the suffrages of the faithful and especially by the acceptable sacrifice of the altar, the holy Synod commands the bishops that they insist that the sound doctrine of purgatory, which has been transmitted by the holy Fathers and the holy Councils, be believed by the faithful of Christ, be maintained, taught, and everywhere preached.[23]

---

21. *Catechism of the Catholic Church* (CCC), 1030–1031.
22. This teaching repeated the previous teaching from the Second Council of Lyons (1274): "Because if they die truly repentant in charity before they have made satisfaction by worthy fruits of penance for sins committed and omitted, their souls are cleansed after death by purgatorial or purifying punishments."
23. Council of Trent, Session 25, *Decree Concerning Purgatory* (December 4, 1563).

Trent continued:

> If anyone shall say that after the reception of the
> grace of justification, to every penitent sinner the
> guilt is so remitted and the penalty of eternal pun-
> ishment so blotted out that no penalty of tempo-
> ral punishment remains to be discharged either in
> this world or in the world to come in purgatory
> before the entrance to the kingdom of heaven can
> be opened: let him be anathema.[24]

For the Heaven-Bound

Based on these definitions, we can summarize the Church's
teaching on purgatory as follows: First, purgatory is for persons who die in God's grace, without mortal sins on their
souls, and are thus destined for heaven. Mortal sins involve
grave matter and the sinner's knowledge and full consent.[25]
These sins are called "mortal" (that is, deadly) because they
expel grace from the soul, precluding it from obtaining union
with God, the source of all life.

In his first epistle, the Apostle John is said to make a distinction between mortal and non-mortal (or "venial") sins.[26]
He writes: "There is sin which is mortal. I do not say that
one is to pray for that. All wrongdoing is sin, but there is sin
which is not mortal." (1 Jn 5:16–17). Those who die with
their mortal sins having been forgiven, or having committed

---

24. Ibid., Session 6, Decree Concerning Justification, Canon 30 (January 13,
    1547). The Church's teaching on purgatory was reaffirmed at the Second
    Vatican Council in Lumen Gentium, No. 49.
25. These would include, for example, the sins of adultery, intentional homi-
    cide, idolatry, and blasphemy.
26. The word "venial" comes from the Latin venia which means pardon or
    forgiveness.

venial sins only, are assured of their place in heaven (although they may have to go to purgatory for final purification).

Thus, purgatory is not for persons who died with unforgiven mortal sin. These souls knowingly chose sin over God during their lives and failed to repent of their sins before death. These are the souls of the reprobate who "will be tormented day and night for ever and ever." (Rev 20:10). Because those in purgatory are guaranteed of their place in heaven, purgatory is a temporary, transitional state between death and eternal life with God.

For Purification and Satisfaction

Secondly, as we have seen, purgatory is a process of purification from sin and of making satisfaction for the debt of punishment due to sin. Even though they have repented of their sins, the Holy Souls still owe God reparation for the damage their sins have caused in accordance with God's standard of justice and equity. Purgatory expiates the temporal punishment due to these sins through the fires of God's divine justice and love.

We will see this clearly when we examine 1 Corinthians 3:15. In this passage, Paul explains how one must pass "through fire" after death before receiving salvation. This process of expiation inflicts the punishment due for the forgiven sins and roots out the defects that moved the soul to sin in the first place. Through this process, the soul achieves the requisite holiness that God requires for it to be suitable for heaven. (Cf. Heb 12:14). We will also examine the biblical passages that teach about making satisfaction to God for the temporal punishments due for our sins, as well as examples of this process found in Scripture.

Relief from Suffrages

A third key Catholic belief about purgatory is that the souls there can have their sufferings lessened, and even be delivered from their torments completely, by the suffrages of those on earth. Suffrages are acts of penance performed by the faithful, such as prayer, fasting and almsgiving. As we will further see in the last chapter, because those in purgatory are members of the one Body of Christ, they can be assisted by other members of the Body on earth.[27] The Apostles' Creed refers to this spiritual relationship as the Communion of Saints, which is an article of faith.

Although God requires from the members of the Body satisfaction for their sins, He doesn't necessarily require it from the member who owes it. God is so merciful that He accepts satisfaction for sin from any member He chooses. As we have seen, this is why Paul can say, "I rejoice in my sufferings for your sake, and in my flesh I complete what is lacking in Christ's afflictions for the sake of his body, that is, the church." (Col 1:24).

By saying that his sufferings are for "your sake" and for "the sake of the body, the church," Paul reveals that one member's suffrages are able to help another member and make up for "what is lacking" in his own suffrages. In other words, God allows one member to merit satisfaction for another member's sins, just as He allowed Christ to atone for the eternal punishment for our sins.

---

27. Cf. 1 Cor 12:12, 27.

What Purgatory Is Not

The foregoing information helps us understand what purgatory is. But it also helps us understand what purgatory is not. This is equally important, because many people have mistaken ideas about purgatory. For example, some people think that purgatory is a place where people get a "second chance" after death to accept God and be saved. Others think that purgatory is an alternative destination for people who are "too good" for hell but "not good enough" for heaven. Some also think that purgatory is a place where the soul works for heaven and gains additional merits from God. These views are erroneous.

Not a "Second Chance"

We are given only one opportunity to respond to God's grace in Christ and accept His mercy—and that is during our earthly lives. This is our only chance to "work out our own salvation with fear and trembling." (Phil 2:12). Once we die, the condition of our souls is fixed and our fate sealed. As Paul says in his letter to the Hebrews, men "die once, and after that comes judgment." (Heb 9:27). Purgatory does not give someone a "second chance" to accept Jesus Christ after he dies.

After He judges us, Christ will no longer "deal with our sins." That is, Christ will no longer give us an opportunity to repent of them and He will no longer forgive them. Once the soul leaves the body in death, the time for clemency and forgiveness has passed. God judges the soul according to the objective state of its condition at the moment of death.

The Church calls Christ's judgment of the soul immediately after death the Particular Judgment. This is the individual judgment that God renders for each and every soul. Paul refers to this judgment when he says, "For we must all appear before the judgment seat of Christ, so that each one may receive good or evil, according to what he has done in the body."[28]

This judgment is to be distinguished from the General Judgment, which will occur at the end of the world when Christ separates the sheep from the goats.[29] At the General Judgment, Christ will simply proclaim publicly each person's Particular Judgment: those who were judged favorably will have their bodies resurrected to eternal life, and those who were judged evil will have theirs resurrected to eternal condemnation.[30]

It is a dreadful thought to think about appearing before the judgment seat of the Lord Jesus Christ to render an account of our sins. The sheer enormity of our many sins, both of commission and omission, should inspire in us a holy fear of God who will hold us accountable for each and every one of them. As Jesus said, "do not fear those who kill the body but cannot kill the soul; rather fear him who can destroy both soul and body in hell."[31]

Not an "Alternative Destination"

Purgatory is not a "middle state" between the place of the saved and the place of the damned. Jesus revealed in Scripture that there are only two ultimate destinations for those who were able to choose good or evil during their lives.

---

28. 2 Cor 5:10. See also Lk 16:22; 23:43 Rom 2:3, 5; 14:10, 12; Heb 9:27; Sir 11:26.
29. Cf. Mt 25:31–46; Jn 5:28–29; 6:40, 44; 12:48; Acts 24:15; 2 Tim 4:8; Rev 20:11–15.
30. Cf. Jn 5:28–29; Rev 20:4–15.
31. Mt 10:28; Lk 12:4–5.

Those who loved God and their neighbors as themselves will "inherit the kingdom prepared for [them] from the foundation of the world." (Mt 25:34). Those who did evil will be thrown "into the eternal fire prepared for the devil and his angels." (Mt 25:41).

Paul reiterates Jesus' teaching: "For he will render to every man according to his works: for those who by patience in well-doing seek for glory and honor and immortality, he will give eternal life; but for those who are factious and do not obey the truth, but obey wickedness, there will be wrath and fury."[32] For those who were given an opportunity to obey God and keep His commandments, Jesus says there will be either "eternal life" or "eternal punishment." (Mt 25:46). Thus purgatory cannot be a third place, that is, an alternative to heaven and hell.

What about Limbo?

The Church throughout the centuries has taught about a third possible destination after death called limbo. Limbo is said to be the eternal resting place for those who die unbaptized but without grievous sin (for example, unbaptized babies). This teaching came about because Scripture is clear that "nothing unclean" shall enter heaven,[33] and all men (through no fault of their own) are born into this world unclean: "Therefore as sin came into the world through one man and death through sin, and so death spread to all men because all men sinned." (Rom 5:12). As we will further see later in the book, this sin which we have all inherited from Adam is called original sin. According to Scripture and Tradition, baptism washes

32. Rom 2:6, 8.
33. Rev 21:27.

away original sin, thereby removing this obstacle to heaven. Jesus taught that baptism is necessary for salvation when He said, "unless one is born of water and the Spirit, he cannot enter the kingdom of God."[34] There are many other Scriptures demonstrating that baptism washes away sin.[35] The rationale for limbo is as follows: Because baptism alone washes away original sin, unbaptized persons cannot go to heaven; however, because God does not punish those who don't commit deliberate sin, unbaptized persons without serious sin do not justly deserve hell. If true, this would necessitate the existence of a third place for these unbaptized souls, which we call limbo (from the Latin word *limbus* meaning "on the margin"). It is the common opinion of the Fathers and doctors of the Church that souls in limbo, although deprived of the Beatific Vision, experience a state of natural happiness.[36]

The doctrine of limbo has been consistently taught throughout the ages, but the Church has never formally elevated limbo to a dogma of the faith.[37] Unlike purgatory,

---

34. Jn 3:5. Cf. Mk 16:16.

35. E.g., Acts 9:18; 22:16; 1 Cor 6:11; Tit 3:5–7; Heb 10:22; 1 Pet 3:21. See also Rom 5:1–5.

36. Two of the greatest Catholic theologians—St. Augustine and St. Thomas Aquinas—believed in limbo, although they disagreed about what the soul experienced there. Augustine said that these souls experience mild punishments while Aquinas and the majority of the saints taught that these souls are not punished at all, but enjoy natural happiness.

37. In addition to the common opinion of the Fathers, saints and doctors of the Church, a number of popes (Pope Siricius [385]; Pope Innocent [414] Pope Zosimus [417]; Pope Innocent III [1201]; Pope John XXII [1321]; Pope Martin V [1417]; Pope Sixtus V [1588]; and, Pope Pius VI [1794]) have denounced the belief that infants who die before baptism enjoy the rewards of eternal life. The Councils of Lyons II (1274) and Florence (1439) both declared that souls who die in original sin (unbaptized) are excluded from the Beatific Vision, but this would not include those souls who had a "baptism of desire" as taught by the Council of Trent (1547). In recent times, Pope Benedict XVI has allowed theologians to investigate the Church's

which was believed by all of the Church Fathers from the very beginning (and which is a dogma of faith), limbo has been advanced as a common theological opinion, but not an infallible dogma.[38] Thus, Catholics are not required to believe in limbo as an article of faith. The Church also urges us to hope for the salvation of unbaptized babies, because God is not bound by His sacraments.[39] Nevertheless, because limbo has been taught by the ordinary Magisterium as well as many great churchmen and theologians over the centuries, it holds significant theological weight and cannot be prudently dismissed, in spite of some human sentiments to the contrary.

While the Bible does not definitively reveal that there is a limbo, this doesn't mean that a third place in the afterlife is inconsistent with Scripture. To the contrary, in Luke's gospel we learn that Lazarus was in "Abraham's bosom," which is sometimes called the "Limbo of the Fathers" or "Hades."[40] Abraham's bosom was the place where the souls of the righteous were detained prior to Jesus' resurrection but which was not heaven.

No soul could go to heaven until Jesus appeased the Father's wrath against sin through His sacrifice on Calvary. Thus, immediately after Jesus died, He descended to Hades

---

traditional teaching on limbo (resulting in no change in the doctrine).

38. Because the doctrine of limbo has been consistently taught by the Church's ordinary Magisterium, it is considered more than a theological hypothesis, but not a *de fide* dogma.

39. The Council of Trent teaches that man is translated from the state of sin to the state of grace "through the laver of regeneration [baptism] or its desire." *Decrees Concerning Justification*, Chapter IV (January 13, 1547). The Church has not defined the parameters of this "desire" (e.g., whether it applies to catechumens only, which is the traditional position; or to infants by virtue of the parents' desire).

40. Cf. Lk 16:22–26. This limbo of the Fathers (*limbus patrum*) is different from the possible limbo of babies (*limbus infantium*), although they may be components of the same spiritual abode.

to inform the righteous souls of their deliverance.[41] This is why the Apostles' Creed says, "He descended into hell (Hades)," which was the realm of the righteous dead. So if Scripture teaches about a place for the righteous dead that was not heaven, then a third place such as purgatory (a place for the righteous dead that is not heaven) is certainly possible. As we will see in the next section, it is not only possible, but a certainty.

Not a Place of Effort and Merit

In purgatory, the soul does none of the work of purification; rather God does all the work. The souls in purgatory have nothing to do because they have already "worked out their own salvation" during their earthly lives. (Cf. Phil 2:12). Their salvation is guaranteed. Scripture is clear that righteous souls are finally freed from their labors. Paul says, "for whoever enters God's rest also ceases from his labors." (Heb 4:10). The angel in the Book of Revelation[42] also says, "Blessed are the dead who die in the Lord henceforth. 'Blessed indeed,' says the Spirit, 'that they may rest from their labors.'" (Rev 14:13).

While the soul rests from its earthly labors, God engages in His heavenly labor of purification. God tests the soul in the fires of His divine love as a refiner does with silver and gold. God says through the prophet Zechariah, "And I will put this third into the fire, and refine them as one refines silver, and test them as gold is tested." (13:9). Malachi also reveals, "For he is like a refiner's fire and like fullers' soap; he will sit as a refiner and purifier of silver, and he will

---

41. Cf. Eph 4:8–9; 1 Pet 3:19; 4:6. See also Acts 2:27, 31; 1 Cor 15:55.
42. The last book of the Bible also goes by the ancient and traditional name of the *Apocalypse*, meaning "unveiling."

purify the sons of Levi and refine them like gold and silver."
(3:2–3). The Book of Proverbs says, "The crucible is for silver, and the furnace is for gold, and the Lord tries hearts."[43]
And we read in Sirach, "For gold is tested in the fire, and
acceptable men in the furnace of humiliation." (2:5).

In addition, it is generally believed that the souls in purgatory are incapable of increasing their merits before God.
Merits are gratuitous gifts that God bestows on the faithful
for obeying His commandments during their lives. These
gifts include an increase in grace, a higher degree of charity,
closer union with the Trinity, and a corresponding increase
in heavenly glory. As Augustine says, when God grants us
merits He is simply crowning His own gifts. Man obtains
from God what God gave man the power to do in the first
place.

In describing how God rewards us with merits, Paul says,
"He who plants and he who waters are equal, and each shall
receive his wages according to his labor." (1 Cor 3:8). The
quality of the labor dictates the quality of the reward (merit).
Paul also says, "For God is not so unjust as to overlook your
work and the love which you showed for his sake in serving
the saints" (Heb 6:10), and, "I seek the fruit which increases
to your credit." (Phi 4:17). The "fruit" symbolizes the
"works" we are called to perform which increase our merits,
or "credits," before God. Jesus also teaches about our need
to bear good fruit to increase our justification before God.[44]

Scripture teaches that the merits we gain on earth are
reserved for our enjoyment in heaven. After the angel in
Revelation praises the souls in heaven who "rest from their
labors," he emphatically proclaims "for their deeds follow

---

43. 17:3. See also 1 Pet 1:6–7; Jude 23; Rev 3:18–19; Dan 12:9–10; Wis 3:5–6.
44. Mt 3:8, 10; 7:16–20; 12:33; 13:23; 21:41, 43; Mk 4:20; Lk 3:8–9; 6:43–44;
8:14–15; 13:6–7, 9; Jn 4:36; 12:24; 15:2,4–5, 8 ,16.

them!" (Rev 14:13). Paul also says that those who are "rich in good deeds, liberal and generous," are "laying up for themselves a good foundation for the future, so that they may take hold of the life which is life indeed." (1 Tim 6:18–19). Our Blessed Lord commanded us, "lay up for yourselves treasures in heaven, where neither moth nor rust consumes and where thieves do not break in and steal."[45]

Of course, because of the immeasurable inequality between God and man, man has no strict right to merit anything from God. As Scripture says, "Who has given a gift to him that he might be repaid?"[46] God owes man nothing. Man can only merit rewards from God because God has freely chosen to associate man with the work of His grace. This relationship between God and man begins at baptism when we become "justified by his grace and become heirs in hope of eternal life." (Tit 3:7).

When we are justified by grace, we become adopted sons of God and heirs of His kingdom. In this new relationship based on grace, we are able to call God "Abba! Father!" (Cf. Gal 4:6–7). Grace makes us children of the Father, and the Father bestows merits upon His children because it is in His nature to do so (not because He has an obligation to do so). As Paul says, we have nothing to boast about before God.[47] All merits from God come solely from God's grace and benevolence, and not from any obligation God has to us. Outside of God's grace, it is impossible to merit anything from God.

We are able to gain merits from God only when our souls are united to our bodies. This is why Paul says that, at our individual judgments, "each one may receive good or evil,

---

45. Mt 6:20. Cf. Mt 19:21; Mk 10:21; Lk 12:33; 18:22.
46. Rom 11:35. Cf. Job 35:7; 41:11.
47. Cf. Rom 2:17, 23; 3:27; 4:2; 11:18; 1 Cor 1:29, 31; 3:21; 4:7; 5:6; 2 Cor 10:17; Eph 2:9.

according to what he has done in the body." (2 Cor 5:10). Once the soul leaves the body—at death—the time for merit has passed. The soul is judged and rewarded (or punished) according to its merits (or demerits).[48] Further, once a person dies, his time for contrition has passed. This is because contrition is a meritorious act which comes from God's grace. Repentance and conversion must happen during this life, when we have the chance.

Speaking of the body, many Protestants say "to be absent from the body is to be present with the Lord." They base their assertion by twisting a statement Paul makes in his Second Letter to the Corinthians. If being absent from the body (death) means being present with the Lord (heaven), then, the Protestant argues, there can be no purgatory.

But this is what Paul actually says: "So we are always of good courage; we know that while we are at home in the body we are away from the Lord, for we walk by faith, not by sight. We are of good courage, and we would rather be away from the body and at home with the Lord." (2 Cor 5:6–8). Paul doesn't say that a soul separated from the body is automatically with the Lord, or that when we die we immediately go to heaven. He simply says we would rather be at home with the Lord than in our bodies. Paul never says a thing about what happens between death and glorification. Moreover, when a soul goes to purgatory, that soul is with the Lord, for it is the Lord who is purifying it for heaven.

Protestants also sometimes refer to Paul's statement in his Letter to the Philippians: "For to me to live is Christ, and to die is gain. If it is to be life in the flesh, that means fruitful labor for me. Yet which I shall choose I cannot tell. I am hard pressed between the two. My desire is to depart and be

---

48. As we will see in 1 Cor 3:12–17, the souls in purgatory are both punished (through purification) and rewarded (with salvation).

with Christ, for that is far better." (1:21–23). Yet, again, Paul is not making a doctrinal statement about what happens to the soul at death. He is simply saying that his desire is to be with Christ rather than labor on earth. Nothing in these verses even remotely addresses the doctrine of purgatory.

What Purgatory May Be

Like heaven and hell, purgatory concerns life after death. Any time we discuss the afterlife, we are dealing with mystery. As Paul says, "For now we see in a mirror dimly, but then face to face. Now I know in part; then I shall understand fully." (1 Cor 13:12). While we know certain things about purgatory from Scripture and Tradition, there are many things we do not know with certainty. For example, we don't know where purgatory is, the exact nature of the sufferings endured there, or how long it lasts. Nevertheless, Scripture and Tradition provide us many clues, as do the private revelations of many saints.

Private, or particular, revelations are revelations that God gives to individuals in the form of visions or apparitions.[49] They are to be distinguished from the public revelation that God has given to the Church in Scripture and Tradition. This public revelation is called the "Deposit of Faith" and includes those truths that are necessary for our salvation. Private revelations—those outside the Deposit of Faith— are based on human testimony, and no Catholic is required to believe in them.

However, when the Church authenticates a private

---

49. A vision is an infusion of knowledge into the understanding of a person so that he can comprehend a mystery. An apparition is an objective phenomenon given by God which has an exterior object. Many saints have received visions and apparitions of purgatory.

revelation of a saint, we cannot dismiss it without offending against reason, for reason demands an assent to the truth when it has been satisfactorily demonstrated. And so in addition to appealing to Scripture and Tradition, we will also occasionally mention some of the many private revelations that holy men and women have received about purgatory. The holiness of these saints is recognized by Christians of all persuasions. Their private revelations, at a minimum, give us abundant spiritual food for thought.[50]

Where Is Purgatory?

As we have seen, the most common phrase describing purgatory is a "place or condition" of temporal punishment after death. While most modern theologians prefer to describe purgatory as a "condition," (or a "state" or "process"), one doesn't err by calling purgatory a "place." When Jesus warned sinners that they would be detained in prison until they paid the last penny (Mt 5:25–26), the early Church interpreted Jesus' warning as a reference to purgatory. Thus, purgatory is a "place" insofar as it detains the soul for purification. Just as the soul was detained in the body during earthly life, the soul may also be detained in the "prison" of purgatory after death.[51]

If purgatory can be called a "place," where is this place? Theologians throughout the centuries have speculated that

---

50. To read about private revelations of purgatory, I recommend *Purgatory—Explained by the Lives and Legends of the Saints*, Fr. F. X. Schouppe, S.J. (TAN Books).

51. Many theologians, including Aquinas, teach that God assigns certain souls a special place of purification on earth, where they sometimes appear to instruct the living or to ask for prayers to lessen their punishments. This may be the cause of apparitions which people witness and are reported by the press from time to time.

purgatory is in the interior of the earth, in the same or similar place as the hell of the damned. This was the position held by Augustine and Aquinas. Only God knows for sure, and there are no compelling arguments on the question. Nevertheless, Scriptures may provide some subtle inferences.

In Matthew's gospel, Jesus says, "so will the Son of Man be three days and three nights in the heart of the earth." (Mt 12:40). As we have seen, when Christ was in the "heart of the earth," He preached deliverance to the souls of the righteous who were waiting for the gates of heaven to be opened for them. These righteous would have included those in purgatory as well, for they were likewise to receive the message of salvation, even though they were making final satisfaction for their sins. If so, this means that purgatory is in the "heart of the earth" where Jesus descended after His death.

In Luke's gospel, even though the rich man was being tormented in Hades, he could still see Lazarus who was in Abraham's bosom, and could communicate with Abraham. (Cf. Lk 16:19–26). Assuming that Abraham's bosom was in the heart of the earth (as shown above), then it is reasonable to conclude that the rich man's place of torment was near or joined to it, separated only by the "great chasm."

While the traditional interpretation is that the rich man is in the hell of the damned, it is possible that he was in purgatory.[52] This is because he still loved his brothers, whereas those in hell no longer have love. He demonstrated love for his brothers by begging Abraham to warn his five brothers of his place of torment (vv. 27–28). If the rich man was in purgatory, then purgatory would be in "the heart of the earth"— the locale of Abraham, Lazarus, and the rest of the righteous dead. (Cf. Mt 12:40).

---

52. This passage was interpreted to be a reference to purgatory in the *Martyrdom of Perpetua and Felicity* and in the writings of Tertullian.

In his letter to the Philippians, Paul says, "at the name of Jesus every knee should bow, in heaven and on earth and under the earth and every tongue confess that Jesus Christ is Lord." (2:10–11). In this verse, Paul is describing the three-fold nature of the Church: the Church Triumphant (in heaven), the Church Militant (on earth) and the Church Suffering (in purgatory). If read literally, which is how Catholics read Scripture unless there is a good reason not to, purgatory would be "under the earth"—that is, within the bowels of the earth's surface.

In the Book of Revelation, John describes those who occupy the earth and the sea, which suggests a continuum of presence on, above, and below the earth's surface: "And I heard every creature in heaven and on earth and under the earth and in the sea, and all therein, saying, 'To him who sits upon the throne and to the Lamb be blessing and honor and glory and might for ever and ever!'" (5:13). This verse hints that those "under the earth" (those in purgatory) are in the subterranean space below the sea, as distinguished from those creatures who are in the sea and on dry land.

It is also reasonable to conclude that God punishes those in the bowels of the earth who loved earthly things over heavenly things. Because man sins by going "down to matter" and not "up to God," a place of punishment in the heart of the earth seems appropriate, whether it's temporal or eternal.[53] Nothing would prevent the all-powerful God from maintaining a hollow in the earth for this purpose. Geologists also believe that fire exists at the earth's core.

---

53. It is plausible to conclude that hell includes or is somehow joined to purgatory, the limbo of the Fathers, and the limbo of babies (if such a place exists). Like the place of the damned, all three of these places are devoid of the Beatific Vision, although the manner of the soul's existence (happiness or sadness) varies greatly.

Scripture also reveals that God punishes sinners in the bowels of the earth. During the reign of Moses, a man named Korah rose up against Moses and his priests (cf. Num 16). Korah and 250 of his followers attempted to confer upon themselves the dignity of the priesthood without the authority of Moses. After Moses pronounced his judgment on the evil actions of Korah and his rebels, God caused the earth to swallow them all alive. Scripture says, "the earth opened its mouth and swallowed them up . . . So they and all that belonged to them went down alive into Sheol; and the earth closed over them, and they perished from the midst of the assembly" (vv. 32–33).

Many saints received revelations that purgatory (and hell) was somewhere in the earth. Saint Teresa had visions of souls coming forth from the depths of the earth and ascending into heaven by the hands of angels. During prayer, Saint Magdalen de Pazzi saw the soul of one of her deceased religious sisters in purgatory come forth from the earth wrapped in a cloak of flames. Saint Frances of Rome was conducted by an angel into both hell and purgatory, which were situated in the bowels of the earth. In Saint Lidwina of Schiedam's vision of purgatory, she saw dungeons, prisons, and other frightening dwellings in the lower regions of the earth.

The Blessed Virgin Mary revealed to three shepherd children (Lucia, Francisco, and Jacinta) in Fatima, Portugal a frightening vision of the happenings in the bowels of the earth.[54] In this vision, the children saw a vast sea of fire with

---

54. The Mother of God appeared to the children six times between May 13 and October 13, 1917. During these appearances, Our Lady affirmed the doctrine of purgatory, along with other core doctrines of the Catholic Faith, and asked that the Pope with the bishops consecrate Russia to her Immaculate Heart. God authenticated these revelations on October 13, 1917 with the "Miracle of the Sun." In this miracle, which was witnessed by 70,000 people, the sun whirled around, emitting brilliant lights which were not harmful

souls appearing like burning embers with human forms. They were floating about in the conflagration and were raised into the air by flames and great clouds of smoke. The children also heard shrieks and groans of pain and despair. Although Lucia later explained that this was a vision of hell, the elements in the vision (fire, flames, smoke, cries) are also consistent with the private revelations that many saints have received about purgatory. This is but a tiny sampling of those visions received by saints suggesting purgatory's existence in the heart of the earth.

How Painful Is Purgatory?

It is generally understood that there are two kinds of pain in purgatory: Pain of sense and pain of loss. The pain of loss consists of being detained from beholding the face of God, the very end for which God created the soul. When the soul was in the body, it struggled between satisfying the desires of the spirit and the desires of the flesh. The Book of Wisdom says, "a perishable body weighs down the soul." (9:15), and Paul repeatedly refers to the tension between body and soul (the flesh and the spirit).[55] When the soul is freed of the body, it seeks God alone. Thus, being deprived of its only desire—God—during its detention in purgatory produces tremendous spiritual torments for the soul, from which it will not be released until it has "paid the last penny." (Mt 5:26).

The pain of sense consists of sensible suffering, akin to

---

to the human eye, and then plunged to the earth before returning to its normal orbit. Since 1930, the Catholic Church has officially recognized the revelations at Fatima.

55. Rom 7:5, 18, 25; 8:3–9, 12–13; 9:8; 1 Cor 3:1, 3; 15:50; Gal 3:3; 5:13, 16–17; 19,24; 6:8, 12–13; Eph 2:3; Col 2:23.

what we would experience in the body. Even though the body is no longer present, God in purgatory allows the soul to experience bodily pain because the sins for which it must make satisfaction were committed "in the body." (2 Cor 5:10). This is why in Luke's gospel the flames could torment the "tongue" of the rich man. Even though he was a disembodied soul, the rich man experienced sensible pain for his sins of gluttony.

In Paul's First Letter to the Corinthians, chapter 3, he describes how God tests the soul after death. Paul reveals that the departed soul "suffers loss" as it is saved "through fire" after God judges the soul. (1 Cor 3:15). We have also seen how Scripture alludes to God using "fire" to purify us like silver and gold. Thus, when read literally, Scripture teaches that the pain of purgatory is the pain of bodily (or "corporeal") fire.

Nevertheless, because the soul is spiritual and fire is material, many Protestants accuse the Catholic interpretation of being unreasonable and illogical. Is it?

Not according to Jesus, who said, "Just as the weeds are gathered and burned with fire, so it will be at the close of the age. The Son of man will send his angels, and they will gather out of his kingdom all causes of sin and all evildoers, and throw them into the furnace of fire; there men will weep and gnash their teeth." (Mt 13:40–42). In this warning, the Lord says that the souls of the accursed will suffer in fire "just as" the weeds are burned with corporeal fire.[56] Far from being an indication that these fires somehow differ,

---

56. The text in Mt 13:40 uses the Greek adverb *houtos* which means "in like manner." This means that the souls of the accursed will burn just like the weeds of the field. The only difference is that the accursed souls "will burn with unquenchable fire" (Mt 3:12). In the third chapter of this book, we will see another critical application of *houtos* found in 1 Cor 3:15.

the Lord strongly indicates that they are the same.

In another warning of the end times, Jesus tells us He will say, "Depart from me, you cursed, into the eternal fire prepared for the devil and his angels." (Mt 25:41). Because the incorporeal demons are currently being punished by the same fire that will receive the bodies of the damned at the end of time it follows that incorporeal souls, like demons, suffer from corporeal fire. This is why Paul says that the departed soul, being tried by the fire of God's justice, "suffers loss" before it obtains its eternal reward. (1 Cor 3:15).

It is also a matter of divine justice that a person who sinned corporeally should also be punished corporeally. The Book of Wisdom says that one "is punished by the very things by which he sins." (11:15). We recall in Luke's gospel how the rich man "feasted sumptuously every day." (16:19). That means he overindulged in the pleasures of the tongue. Thus it's no surprise when he begs Abraham to send Lazarus to cool his tongue with water (v. 24).

Saints over the centuries have given us frightening revelations of the pains of purgatory. They have seen visions of violent flames, lava, hot chains, and irons punishing the souls of the just. They have heard screams and cries of agony and fury as the souls endured the fires of expiation. Those graced with these visions have all said that the chastisements of purgatory are beyond our comprehension, surpassing all the sufferings of this life. If a temporal fire causes a painful burn to the skin in this life, how much more pain does a divine flame cause the soul in purgatory? It is a sobering meditation.

Venerable Bede reports a vision of purgatory consisting of deep cavern of fire on one side and ice and snow on the other. The souls would violently toss themselves back and forth between the fire and ice, between one torture and the other. As soon as a soul could no longer endure the flames, it plunged itself into the ice and snow, only to return to the fire, and then back to the ice and so forth, never to find repose. Job reveals this punishment as he speaks of God's judgment: "Let him pass from the snow waters to excessive heat, and his sin even to hell."[57] The Greek word for "hell" is Hades, the place of detention for departed souls.

In the Book of Revelation, Jesus threatened to punish Jezebel for her sin of adultery by throwing her "on a sick bed" where she committed her sins. (2:22). The heavens also cry, "Render to her as she herself has rendered, and repay her double for her deeds; mix a double draught in the cup she mixed. As she glorified herself and played the wanton, so give her a like measure of torment and mourning." (18:6–7). The prophet Hosea also reveals that sinners "became detestable like the thing they loved." (9:10). This comes right before Hosea's warning in the previous verse: "he will remember their iniquity, he will punish their sins" (v. 9). Ezekiel also reveals, "their silver and gold are not able to deliver them in the day of the wrath of the Lord; they cannot satisfy their hunger or fill their stomachs with it. For it was the stumbling block of their iniquity; therefore I will make it an unclean thing to them."[58]

As we alluded to, the great minds of the Church agree that the least pain in purgatory surpasses the greatest pain of earthly life.[59] Regarding pain of sense, because punishment is inflicted upon the soul directly which is the source of all bodily sensations, it follows that this pain of sense is worse than anything the soul could experience in the body. The severity of the punishment, of course, depends upon

---

57. Job 24:19 (DR). See also Ps 65:10, 12.
58. Ezek 7:19–20. See also Isa 27:7–8; 28:17.
59. Many have held this position including Augustine, Gregory, Chrysostom, Bede, Anselm, Bernard, Aquinas, and Bellarmine.

the severity of the sins, for the Lord says, "I will recompense them according to their deeds." (Jer 25:14). The Lord also says that a man is punished "in proportion to his offense." (Deut 25:2).

Regarding pain of loss, the more something is desired the more painful is its absence. Since the soul in purgatory desires God alone and with the most intense desire, it follows that this pain of loss is worse than anything the soul could experience while on earth. The Fathers and Doctors of the Church agree that this pain of loss of the vision of God is the greatest pain of purgatory.

Notwithstanding the supreme pains of purgatory, the souls there freely submit to their punishments out of their fervent love and desire for God. They would rather undergo these terrible torments than appear before God with their current defects. They love God above all things, for their disembodied souls seek Him alone. Furthermore, because God loves those He chastises,[60] He gives the souls in purgatory great consolations. Although God wants us to have a holy fear of sin and punishment, He wants us to temper that fear with great trust in His mercy, for God's mercy is as infinite as His justice. Thus, while their sufferings are like those of hell, their consolations give them a taste of heaven.[61]

---

60. Cf. Heb 12:6.

61. For example, Catherine of Genoa said that God overwhelms the Holy Souls with such love that it would annihilate them if they were not immortal. As Magdalen de Pazzi witnessed her brother suffering in purgatory, she also noted his great happiness and satisfaction. Stanislaus of Cracow learned from a soul he raised from the dead, that the soul preferred to return to the torments of purgatory than to risk losing his soul by remaining in this life. Catherine de Ricci, whom God allowed to suffer purgatorial punishments for a certain prince, reported that we endure the excesses of purgatory with great peace and love. Bridget of Sweden, and many other saints, also reveal that the Blessed Virgin Mary and the angels mitigate the chastisements of purgatory.

How Long Does Purgatory Last?

Although we don't know exactly how time operates in the afterlife, it seems clear that souls are detained in purgatory "for a time."[62] Jesus' warning that we will not get out of the prison of purgatory until we have paid the last penny means we are detained for a period of time. (Mt 5:25–26). Of course, one person's debt may be larger or smaller than another's. This means the "time" for making payment (satisfying the debt of sin) will be longer for some than it will be for others.

The rich man in Hades was being tormented over a period of time, during which he expressed his anguish, asked for mercy and relief of his suffering, and begged for his brothers to be warned about his place of torment. The purgatorial pain of loss exists during the time in which the soul cannot see God, and ceases at the time of the soul's deliverance. How time is calculated after death we don't know for sure. But it is reasonable to presume that the suffering is not instantaneous. To the soul's perception it endures for a "time"—for some souls, a very long time.

In his first letter to the Corinthians (which we will examine in more detail in the third chapter), Paul uses metaphors to describe a person's works and how God judges those works after the person dies. Good works are symbolized by "gold, silver, precious stones" and bad works by "wood, hay, and stubble." (3:12). Paul reveals that after death God judges with fire the type of work each person has done while on earth. Those who have built with gold, silver, and precious stones receive their heavenly reward (v. 14). Because the fire cannot consume these elements, they (the good works) accompany

---

62. Some theologians refer to this transitional period as "aeviternity," which is understood as the mean between time and eternity.

the person into heaven. Those who have built with wood, hay, and stubble have a different outcome. Paul reveals that these materials (sins) are "burned up" in the fire. (1 Cor 3:15). As we will later see, the person who built with these bad materials must also pass through the same fire before receiving salvation (v. 15). Thus, as the fire consumes the bad materials, it punishes the person who built with them.

The fire consumes these elements, and at different speeds. Why? Because wood remains longer in fire than hay or stubble. Hay and stubble burn more quickly, and wood burns more slowly. Paul's metaphorical usage of these elements demonstrates the obvious: some sins are more grievous than others. Thus, some sins are punished longer and more severely in purgatory than others. Those who had graver sins (represented by wood) will be purified longer than those with lesser sins (represented by stubble). The severity of punishment corresponds to a person's guilt, while the length of punishment corresponds to how deeply the sin has taken root in his soul.

So how long does this purification take? Well, in this life, we know that times of enjoyment appear to pass quickly while times of suffering seem long. The more intense the suffering, the longer it seems for time to pass. Many saints who have received revelations about purgatory have written about how the poor souls experience time. Their conclusions are unanimous: the shortest time in purgatory seems to be an extraordinarily, excessively long time. Hence, like the pains of sense and loss, this pain of duration (length of time) is intensified beyond anything we have experienced in this life. In fact, it is because the sufferings of purgatory (sense and loss) are so incredibly intense that the soul perceives time as it does.

One brief and very average account will suffice. The

Dominican friar and bishop St. Antoninus records the story of a sick man who was given a choice by his guardian angel: either to die immediately and spend three days in purgatory, or to bear his illness for one more year and then go directly to heaven. The man chose purgatory. After one hour, his angel visited him in purgatory. The man complained to his angel that he had agreed to three days only but had been suffering in the purgatorial flames for several years. When the angel informed him that he had been in purgatory for only one hour, the surprised soul begged his angel to bring him back to earth where he would be willing to suffer as long as God willed.

This private revelation and others like it are consistent with the opinions of the Fathers and Doctors of the Church. Robert Bellarmine, for example, said that the pains of purgatory seem to last not only ten and twenty years, but in some cases entire centuries. When the seer Lucia at Fatima asked the Blessed Mother about her deceased friend Amelia (who died at eighteen or twenty years of age), the Mother of God said, "she will be in purgatory until the end of the world."[63] It is likely that even righteous people will have to expiate their venial sins and bad habits in purgatory. As Scripture says, "a righteous man falls seven times" in one day. (Prov 24:16). How long will a righteous man have to suffer in purgatory? And how does this suffering compare to that of an unrighteous man? Although it is impossible to calculate with precision how long we would have to suffer in purgatory, the effort at least gives us something to think about.

Indeed, if people really contemplated the reality of suffering excruciating torments for a very long time after death, they would repent and amend their lives. A reasonable person

---

63. May 13, 1917.

would rather endure a deadly disease or forsake an abundant fortune in this short life rather than suffer the unfathomable pains of purgatory in the next life. If we cannot imagine enduring physical sufferings for ten or thirty or fifty years, how much more incomprehensible are the spiritual sufferings of purgatory? Surely, if we really knew (as did so many saints through private revelations), we would suffer the most severe penances in this world to avoid them in the world to come. In the last chapter, we will discuss how to avoid purgatory, as we unite our sufferings with the Cross of our Lord Jesus Christ.

Before we close this chapter, we must emphasize the following: God does not want us to go to purgatory. No, we impose purgatory on ourselves. Our Lord has told us, "my yoke is easy, and my burden is light." (Mt 11:30). If we love God with all our heart, mind, soul, and strength,[64] we have nothing to fear. The Apostle John teaches us that "we may have confidence for the day of judgment" if we keep God's commandments and do what pleases Him. (1 Jn 4:17). As we will see in the next chapter, we can do these things only by grace. The way we respond to God's grace in this life will determine the outcome of the next. Our Lord loves us and will consume us in the fire of His love. (Cf. Heb 12:29). Whether that will include a stop in purgatory is our choice.

With the foregoing information as background, let us now examine in more detail the Scriptural evidence for Purgatory.

---

64. Cf. Mt 22:37; Mk 12:30; Lk 10:27.

SATISFACTION FOR SIN

O THIS point, we have learned that purgatory is a place or condition of temporal punishment for souls who are going to heaven but have not made sufficient satisfaction for their sins while on earth. The sinner incurs punishment for forgiven mortal and venial sins, for unforgiven venial sins, and for any dross remaining in the soul. The Lord reveals through Isaiah, "I will clean purge away thy dross, and I will take away all thy tin." (1:25). In purgatory, God exacts from the soul the remaining satisfaction owed to Him as He purifies the soul from its sins and evil inclinations and prepares it for heaven.

Why God Demands Satisfaction

"Satisfaction" can be understood as compensation for injury inflicted. When a creature transgresses the laws of the Creator (that is, commits sin), he injures his relationship with God. This injury results in an inequality opposed to friendship with God as well as an inequality of justice. The word "equality" in our discussion means there is an "equation" between God and man according to the divine order established by God. When man throws the equation out of balance by sinning, God requires him to restore the balance as a matter of justice. The sinner does this by making satisfaction.

Hence, God wills us to endure temporal punishments as satisfaction for sin because His perfect justice and holiness demand it. Sin is a transgression against the order of divine justice with which God governs the universe. Sin offends God who has "arranged all things by measure and number and weight."[65] The prophet cries, "Correct me, O Lord, but in just measure; not in thy anger, lest thou bring me to nothing." (Jer 10:24). God requires a just measure of satisfaction to restore His divine order, "For the Lord is a God of justice"[66] and "he judges the peoples with equity." (Ps 9:8). Just as God willed Christ to counterbalance the eternal consequences of sin through His infinite satisfaction (His death on the Cross), He wills us to satisfy the temporal consequences of sin through our finite satisfactions.

Satisfaction, then, is the act of punishment inflicted by God and incurred by sinners which restores the equality of friendship and justice between them. This punishment heals our past sins, but it also preserves us from future sins because man is not inclined to fall into the sin for which he has suffered punishment. This means satisfaction has two components: penal compensation (for past sins) and willful preservation (from future sins).[67] Satisfaction means giving

---

65. Wis 11:20; cf. Prov 16:11; Isa 27:8; Mt 7:2.
66. Isa 30:18.
67. We say "willful" because avoiding sins in the future involves the free will's refusal to sin. Unlike the body, which can be preserved from sickness by removing the causes of sickness, the free will is not necessarily preserved from spiritual sickness (sin) even when the causes of sin are removed (through punishment). Similarly, the free will can choose to avoid sin even when the causes of sin are present (e.g., internal or external temptations).

to God the due honor we owe Him. It is demanded by justice and inspired by charity.

In philosophy, we call satisfaction a "contrary movement" that restores the natural, moral, and divine order.[68] Satisfaction requires a movement contrary to that which one wishes. This is why when one abuses his freedom (through crime), his freedom is taken away (in prison). Or to return to our earlier example: damaging someone's car is the first movement; paying to repair the car is the contrary movement that renders satisfaction. If I damaged my neighbor's car and did not make satisfaction to my neighbor through an act that is contrary to my wish, a judge can force me to do so. He can order me to pay, or, if I am unable to pay, he can punish me by throwing me into prison. In either of these scenarios, satisfaction is rendered both to punish my offense and to preserve me from future offenses.

It is no different with God. When we sin—which is always an offense against God—we must make satisfaction to God to repair the relationship we have injured.[69] We must reestablish the equality of justice and friendship with God. David recognized this necessity when he said, "What shall I render to the Lord for all his bounty to me?" (Ps 116:12). We must suffer a movement that is contrary to our sinful desire to eliminate the imbalance we have created. Although Christ atoned for the eternal penalty, God requires us to make satisfaction for the temporal penalties. If we don't make sufficient satisfaction to God for our sins in this life, we will have to do so in the next. The Supreme Lawgiver and Judge will detain us until we have fully paid our debt to Him.

---

68. This is the philosophy of the Angelic Doctor, St. Thomas Aquinas.

69. Our ability to make satisfaction for sin comes from God's grace and not our own initiative. This means that our works of satisfaction our really God's works by virtue of His grace working within us (cf. Phil 2:13).

Temporal Versus Eternal Punishment

We can understand the difference between temporal and eternal punishment, and its relation to sin, in the following way: If a person completely turns away (through mortal sin) from the infinite good that is God, there is a corresponding infinite punishment (endured in hell). If a person turns to a mutable good beyond right reason (venial sin), there is a finite punishment (endured here or in purgatory). The punishment is finite (temporal) because the good itself is finite and because the person hasn't turned away from God completely. That is, the person hasn't ultimately chosen the mutable good over the immutable good. Hence, venial sins incur temporal punishment, while mortal sins incur eternal punishment.

When a person incurs eternal punishment (hell), he needs a satisfaction of infinite value to be released from his punishment. Of course, only God who has infinite power is able to provide infinite satisfaction. This He gave in the Person of Jesus Christ, an eternal being without sin. Man avails himself of Christ's atoning work by confessing his sins. The Apostle John says, "If we confess our sins, he is faithful and just, and will forgive our sins and cleanse us from all unrighteousness." (1 Jn 1:9).

The Apostle John also records in his Gospel that Christ intends this forgiveness to be granted in the Sacrament of Confession. Jesus instituted this sacrament when He declared to His apostles, "If you forgive the sins of any, they are forgiven; if you retain the sins of any, they are retained." (Jn 20:23). The apostles handed on this authority to their successors through "the laying on of hands."[70] The people

---

70. Cf. Acts 6:5–6; 13:2–3; 14:22; 1 Tim 4:14; 5:22; 2 Tim 1:6.

in Jesus' time marveled at the fact that God had given this authority "to men." (Mt 9:8).

In confession, God forgives the sinner by virtue of Christ's atoning work. However, if the man falls again into grave sin, "there no longer remains a sacrifice for sins" until he confesses his new sins. (cf. Heb 10:26). That is why John reveals that God's forgiveness is conditional upon the sinner's willingness to seek that forgiveness in confession: "If we confess, then he will forgive our sins." (Cf. 1 Jn 1:9). When the sinner confesses his sins, God applies Christ's "sacrifice" to the sinner to forgive those "sins." After confession, Paul explains, "Where there is forgiveness of these, there is no longer any offering for sin." (Heb 10:18). By this Paul means that, when sin is forgiven, the efficacy of Christ's atoning work for that sinner has been accomplished. This is why Peter says that man "was cleansed from his old sins." (2 Pet 1:9).

When a person incurs finite punishment, he needs a finite satisfaction, that is, one of proportionate value, to be released. Although Christ is the source of all forgiveness and satisfaction, God requires man to play his part. Man, with finite power, can offer finite satisfaction to God to atone for his sins. These are the "spiritual sacrifices" we offer to God through Jesus Christ by virtue of our baptism.[71] How can we be certain of this? We can be certain because we know that man can make satisfaction to another man (by an apology, a gift, or other type of sacrifice). Therefore, man can also make satisfaction to God, for God is more merciful than man.

When a person dies, his debt of punishment is not automatically discharged. This makes logical sense. If someone intentionally tortures and kills ten innocent people, and dies without repentance, he will be punished forever in hell. If

---

71. See 1 Pet 2:5; see also Rom 12:1; Phil 4:18; 2 Tim 4:6; Heb 13:15.

the same person dies shortly after committing the murders, but repents on his deathbed, God forgives him of his eternal punishment, but he doesn't get off scot-free. He doesn't just waltz into heaven. He must make satisfaction for his grievous sins. God is infinite mercy, but He is also infinite justice. If the person did not make satisfaction during his earthly life, he will do so in purgatory. As Paul warns us, "Do you suppose you will escape the judgment of God?" (Rom 2:3).

Satisfaction and God's Anger

In Scripture, God reveals His will to restore the equity of justice by expressing His anger toward sin. Unlike human anger, which is often motivated by selfish pride and revenge, God's anger is simply His objective judgment of evil and sin. The scriptures do not attribute to God the quality of human anger because human anger is an emotion and God does not have emotions or passions. However, Scripture's descriptions of God's anger are not mere anthropomorphisms (that is, projecting human qualities onto God) because God really expresses His displeasure with and punishes sin. Thus, Scripture attributes anger to God analogically or metaphorically, meaning that divine anger is analogous to, but also different from, human anger.

Because God's anger is an expression of His divine judgment against sin, His anger is always ordered to the good. Sin violates God's justice and disregards His honor and holiness; it is an an affront to His very nature. In fact, God was so opposed to the sin of Adam that He condemned the entire human race to death and condemnation. (Cf. Rom 5:12). To offset the infinite insult of Adam's sin, Jesus Christ voluntarily offered Himself in sacrifice to avert the Father's anger and satisfy His justice. This is why Scripture says that

God "sent his Son to be a propitiation for our sins."[72]
Propitiation refers to the process by which God's anger is appeased and His justice satisfied through sacrifice. Scripture reveals how, throughout salvation history, God appeases His own anger by sending sinners temporal punishments. For example, through Ezekiel, God says, "Thus shall my anger spend itself, and I will vent my fury upon them and satisfy myself; and they shall know that I, the Lord, have spoken in my jealousy, when I spend my fury upon them." (5:13). In this passage, God is not referring to the eternal penalty of hell; He's referring to the temporal penalties that He imposed upon the Israelites for their sins, which included war, famine, robbery, animal attacks, desecration of holy places, dispersion, and death.[73] God sent these punishments to appease His anger (in other words, to satisfy His justice), so that God could later say, "So will I satisfy my fury on you, and my jealousy shall depart from you; I will be calm, and will no more be angry."[74]

The scriptures are also full of many examples where people propitiate God's anger through acts of penance and sacrifice and mitigate or eliminate God's ensuing punishments.[75] In the Old Testament, we see this with the sacrifices of Noah, Job, Moses, and David. In the New Testament, Christ Himself commands us to "bear fruits that befit repentance" (Lk 3:8). Thus, even though Jesus is the ultimate propitiation for sin, He requires us to appease God through our own sacrifices. This is why Paul can rejoice in completing what is lacking in Christ's sufferings through his own sacrifices. (Col

---

72. 1 Jn 4:10 (DR); see also Heb 2:17; 1 Jn 2:2 (DR).
73. Cf. Ezek 5:10–17; 6:4; 7:22; Isa 10:16.
74. 16:42; cf. Ezek 21:17.
75. Job 42:7–10; Gen 18:22–33; Ex 4:24–26; 32:14; Num 25:11–13; Deut 9:18–19; 1 Chron 21:14–27.

1:24). This is also why Paul can say that he will "gladly spend and be spent for your souls." (2 Cor 12:15) and that he is "already on the point of being sacrificed." (2 Tim 4:6). If we fail to make up for what we owe in this life through sacrifice, we will make satisfaction in the next life through suffering.

This means it is erroneous for Protestants to reject purgatory and the need for temporal punishments on the ground that Christ "paid the legal debt for our sins." It's true that if sin were a legal debt that Christ fully paid, purgatory would be unnecessary. But then so would hell. That is because God would not require one payment from Christ and a second payment from the sinner, both for the same sin. That would violate the law of justice. If Christ really satisfied the debt, there is no more debt to owe—and we all go to heaven.

Thus, Christ's sacrifice is not an impersonal legal motion to a judge to pardon the criminal, but a personal, intimate plea to the Father to forgive the sinner. Christ's atonement is about personal propitiation, not legal payment. It is about grace, not law, for Paul says, "you are not under law but under grace." (Rom 6:14).

Catholics also point out that Christ's work is not a "legal transaction" because in order to be saved one must accept the "payment" through an act of faith. Scripture clearly teaches that God requires the sinner to have faith in Christ's blood for it to benefit him. (Rom 3:25). The problem, then, with the Protestant understanding is that faith is not a dimension of law. One doesn't need to have "faith" in a criminal court judge to issue a punishment when the law is violated. A defendant's "faith" is irrelevant to his sentence. Rather, faith is a dimension of relationships, particularly within a family. This is why it is impossible to enter the New Covenant without faith. (Cf. Heb 11:6). Protestants have no explanation for why faith is required if Christ's atonement is a mere legal transaction. This is why Scripture always puts Christ's atoning work in the context of family, not law.

For example, Paul says that Christ was sent "to redeem those who were under the law, so that we might receive adoption as sons." (Gal 4:5). Paul also says, "He destined us in love to be his sons through Jesus Christ" (Eph 1:5) and "for in Christ Jesus you are all sons of God, through faith." (Gal 3:26). Christ's atonement doesn't release defendants from a judge, but reconciles sons to their Father. This is the heart of the story of the Prodigal Son. (Cf. Lk 15:3–32). Because we are adopted sons of God, Paul says, "God has sent the Spirit of his Son into our hearts, crying, 'Abba! Father!' So through God you are no longer a slave but a son, and if a son then an heir." (Gal 4:6–7). We will say more about the Protestant view of the atonement later in this chapter.

Satisfaction as an Act of Mercy

God doesn't impose punishment upon sinners solely because it appeases His anger and is demanded by His justice. He also imposes temporal punishments upon us to further His work of saving our souls.

After all, God "desires all men to be saved and to come to the knowledge of the truth."[76] Temporal punishment aids the sinner's reformation by moving the sinner to repentance, which is necessary for salvation. Justice aims not only

---

76. 1 Tim 2:4. Aquinas teaches that God antecedently (absolutely) wills all men to be saved, prior to considering the whole of humanity and the good of the universe; and, consequently (simply) wills to permit some men to be damned because their damnation reflects God's avenging justice which is a good that would not be communicated to the whole of humanity and the universe if every single person were saved. In other words, God wishes to communicate His goodness to humanity in the greatest measure, which is done by manifesting both His mercy and His justice, and not His mercy alone.

at removing inequality already existing, but also safeguarding equality for the future. Since satisfaction is an act of justice, it is both punitive and rehabilitative. This means that God's requirement for satisfaction is an act of mercy as well.

Throughout the Old Testament, God sent many spiritual and material chastisements upon the Jews to move them to repentance. God does the same in the New Testament. Paul says, "For godly grief produces a repentance that leads to salvation." (2 Cor 7:10). Thus, punishment is both penal and medicinal. It's like when someone gets physically sick for abusing his body through overeating or lack of exercise. Just as these warning signs move people to "repent" of their unhealthy lifestyles and get back on the road to health, God sends spiritual chastisements to produce the same effect in our spiritual lives.

Temporal punishment is also medicinal because it helps us grow in holiness. As we will see below, our battle against evil and temptation is itself a temporal punishment for sin. After Paul refers to the Hebrews' "struggle against sin,"[77] he says that God our Father "disciplines us for our good, that we may share his holiness. For the moment all discipline seems painful rather than pleasant; later it yields the peaceful fruit of righteousness to those who have been trained by it." (Heb 12:10–11). Paul then says to "strive for . . . the holiness without which no one will see the Lord" (v. 14).

Therefore this struggle against sin—which is a punishment for sin—helps produce the very holiness that we need to get to heaven. Paul directly connects our suffering for sin with our salvation. We are made perfect through suffering because Jesus, the pioneer of our salvation, was perfected in suffering.[78] Thus, in his letter to the Romans, Paul says

---

77. Heb 12:4.
78. Cf. Heb 2:10; 12:2.

we are sons of God, "provided we suffer with him in order that we may also be glorified with him." (Rom 8:17). Again, Paul teaches that our glorification depends upon our sanctification through suffering—which will occur in this life or the next.

The story of the boy who broke his neighbor's window gives us a good perspective. The boy's father paid his neighbor the full price for the repair, but still required his son to earn money to contribute to the cause. This was painful for the boy but kept him in his father's good graces. The discipline taught the boy the value of money and the meaning of hard work. It also taught the boy that there are consequences for his actions and that he should avoid breaking windows in the future. In short, the father's discipline helped conform his son to his own likeness (a man who knows the value of money and hard work, and has respect for other people's property). If the boy failed to make his contribution as his father required, he would be alienated from his father and his father's full payment for the repair would avail him nothing.

As applied here, the father represents Jesus Christ and the son represents all of us. Christ paid the "full price" for our sins (by satisfying for the eternal punishment), but He requires us to contribute as well (by helping to satisfy for temporal punishment). Our sins have created an inequality of justice for which satisfaction is required. We have failed to recognize God's holiness and our sinfulness. Restoring us to God's friendship by suffering temporal punishments keeps us in God's good graces, helps us avoid sin, and conforms us to the image of His Son. If we fail to make satisfaction for our sins as God requires, we will be alienated from Him, and Christ's "payment" will avail us nothing.

Scripture teaches that God has predestined us to holiness precisely by being "conformed to the image of his son."

(Rom 8:29). As Scripture says, "For the Lord disciplines him whom he loves, and chastises every son whom he receives. It is for discipline that you have to endure. God is treating you as sons; for what son is there whom his father does not discipline?" (Heb 12:6–7). Being conformed to Christ means suffering and dying with Him so that we will be raised to life with Him.[79] This is why Paul says, "while we live we are always being given up to death for Jesus's sake, so that the life of Jesus may be manifested in our mortal flesh." (2 Cor 4:11). Just as Christ "learned obedience through what he suffered,"[80] we too must learn obedience by suffering. Though Christ was sinless, He suffered for our sins—and so too must we.

This means that we can use the sufferings of the present life to satisfy for our sins. This is why Paul tells us to "rejoice in our sufferings," for sufferings produce the endurance and character we need to make it to heaven. (Rom 5:3). Even though the scourges of this life are not in our control, they acquire a satisfactory character if we accept them with the intention of making satisfaction. This is why faithful Catholics deal with suffering by saying, "Offer it up." In fact, offering our sufferings up to God for our sins does bring the sufferings within our power, since we bear them patiently and transform them into meritorious and satisfactory works. On the other hand, suffering borne impatiently and without faith in God will worsen a sinner's condition, meriting him neither satisfaction nor grace.

God's temporal punishments are merciful in another way: they serve as a warning to others not to fall into sin. Paul makes this clear in his First Letter to the Corinthians when he explains how the Jews were overcome by all kinds of evils

---

79. Cf. Rom 6:5; 2 Tim 2:11; see also 2 Cor 1:5; 1 Pet 2:21.
80. Heb 8:5.

because of their sins. After Paul recalls the Jews' punishment during the Exodus in the desert, he says, "Now these things are warnings for us, not to desire evil as they did." (10:6). A few verses later, after Paul recalls the Jews' punishment for idolatry and sexual immorality, he again says, "Now these things happened to them as a warning, but they were written down for our instruction, upon whom the end of the ages has come" (v. 11). The Book of Proverbs also says, "The wicked man being scourged, the fool shall be wiser."[81] God imposes temporal punishments upon us to bring us—and others—to eternal salvation.

Examples of Temporal Punishment

Scripture provides many examples where God imposes temporal punishments upon people after forgiving their sins. For example, after Cain kills his brother Abel, God punishes Cain by cursing the ground that he regularly tilled. God reveals to Cain that when he now tilled the ground, it would no longer yield fruit. (Gen 4:13). God also punishes Cain by making him a fugitive and a wanderer on the earth (v. 13). Cain's temporal punishment suited his crime of fratricide; he is punished by the very ground that received his brother's blood. Yet the prideful Cain has the nerve to respond to God, "My punishment is greater than I can bear" (v. 13).

We mentioned the sins of the people of Israel and the temporal punishments God sends them for those sins (war, famine, disease, and death). In addition to grumbling against God about their exile in the desert, the Jews' gravest sin during the Exodus was worshiping the golden calf.[82] God forgives the Jews' sin of idolatry, but, in addition to

---

81. 19:25 (DR).
82. Ex 32:4–8.

killing some of them and afflicting them with a plague,[83] He also punishes them by prohibiting them from seeing the Promised Land.[84]

That temporal punishment was also perfectly suited to the sin. The Israelites committed idolatry in the desert because they lacked patience and trust in God. In satisfaction for their sin, God punishes them in the desert, which requires them to have even more patience with and trust in God—another forty years worth![85] In other words, God sought to restore the Israelites to the equality of justice by imposing a punishment upon them that was directly contrary to their will.

Most of us also know the story about King David. David sins against God by committing adultery with Bathseba and murdering Uriah the Hittite.[86] God forgives David's sins, but punishes him by taking the life of the child he conceived in adultery, and by allowing his wives to be raped.[87] Because David took the innocent life of Uriah, God takes the innocent life of David's child; because David committed adultery with Bathsheba, God has David's wives commit adultery—two acts that are contrary to what David would have naturally wished.

Some Protestants argue that God kills David's child and has his wives violated, not to inflict temporal punishment upon him, but to redress the public scandal caused by his sin (vv. 12–14). This argument is short-sighted. First, redressing

---

83. Ex 32:28, 35.
84. Num 14:21–23, 30, 32, 35. Out of a million Jews who crossed the Red Sea, God allowed only Joshua and Caleb to see the Promised Land.
85. Cf. Num 14:34. God chooses the temporal punishment of forty years to coincide with the Israelites forty days of spying out the Promised Land, which showed their lack of faith and trust in God.
86. 2 Sam 12:9–10.
87. 2 Sam 12:14, 18–19.

public scandal, insofar as it warns the public not to com~ mit the sin, is one of the reasons why God imposes tempo~ ral punishment. Secondly, that David wept, fasted, and laid prostrate on the ground for seven days and was forgiven by God demonstrates that David's actions made some satisfac~ tion for his sin (vv. 16–17). Finally, that David repented of his sin and wrote Psalms 32 and 51 shows that the temporal punishments he endured brought about his reformation.

In the New Testament, we see how the Corinthians sinned grievously by receiving the Eucharist unworthily. Paul warned them that receiving the body and blood of Christ in mortal sin would result in eternal punishment when he declared, "Whoever, therefore, eats the bread or drinks the cup of the Lord in an unworthy manner will be guilty of pro~ faning the body and blood of the Lord"; "For any one who eats and drinks without discerning the body eats and drinks judgment upon himself."[88]

However, Paul also told the Corinthians that because of their sacrilege they were suffering temporal punishments of weakness and illness: "That is why many of you are weak and ill, and some have died." (1 Cor 11:30). Because the Corinthians abused the flesh of Christ in the Eucharist, God punished their own flesh with sickness and death.[89] This is another example of God's desire to restore the equality of justice between Himself and His creatures.

To the Romans, Paul reveals, "There will be tribulation and distress for every human being who does evil." (Rom 2:9). The one who "does evil" commits the sin, and the "tribulation

---

88. 1 Cor 11:27, 30.
89. Death is a temporal punishment because we will be resurrected from the dead (2 Macc 7:14; 12:43; Dan 12:2; Mt 22:23, 28, 30–31; Mk 12:23; Lk 14:14; Lk 20:27, 33, 35–36; Jn 5:29; 11:24–25; Acts 24:15, 21; Rom 6:5; 1 Cor 15:12–13, 21, 42; Phil 3:11; 2 Tim 2:18; Heb 6:2; 11:35; Rev 20:5–6)..

and distress" the sinner experiences are the punishments for his sin. Scripture makes it clear that sin (the act) and punishment (the guilt) are two different things. As we said above, every sin incurs the guilt of punishment, even after the sin is forgiven. God removes the "guilt of their sin" only after the sinner makes satisfaction.[90] Thus, after the angel touched Isaiah's lips with a hot, burning coal, he declared, "your guilt is taken away, and your sin forgiven." (Isa 6:7).

Temporal Punishment and Remnants of Sin

God does not limit temporal punishment to our actual sin. We also experience temporal punishments from the Original Sin of Adam. These temporal penalties are often referred to as the "remnants of sin." The remnants of sin include the soul's spiritual inclination to sin, which the Church calls "concupiscence." The remnants of sin refer also to the dispositions in the soul caused by the acts that precede actual sin (for example, greed or lust). Even after the sin is forgiven, these dispositions to sin remain. In fact, because actual sin stokes and kindles the concupiscence, these dispositions are often stronger after the will has given in to them. Scripture says, "he who despises small things will fail little by little." (Sir 19:1). This heightened proclivity to evil is a sure sign of a temporal punishment with which God has burdened our very nature.

To understand the remnants from actual sin, we may consider how God heals the sinner. Sometimes God does it suddenly, such as when He immediately made the leper clean[91] or instantly cured the Gentile woman's daughter. (Mt 15:28). A great example occurs in the Gospel of Luke,

---

90. Jer 33:8; see also Ps 32:5; Isa 27:9; Jer 2:22; 30:14–15; Ezek 18:24; Hos 12:8.
91. Cf. Mt 8:3.

when Jesus completely pardons the sinful woman. (Lk 7:47–48). However, sometimes God heals the sinner in degrees. In Mark's Gospel, we read how Jesus restores the blind man to imperfect sight when the man says, "I see men; but they look like trees, walking." (8:24). Then Jesus restores him perfectly, after which he "saw everything clearly" (v. 25).

Jesus's initial healing of the blind man signifies the forgiveness of his sin. The imperfect vision that remained after the forgiveness signifies the remnants of his sin. Even though the sinner is restored to grace, he retains the vestiges of his past sins, which need further healing. Both the debt of punishment and the remnants of sin—itself a temporal punishment for sin—leave a stain on the soul that impedes its complete union with God until removed by God.

Scripture refers to the remnants of sin as a "stain" on the soul: "Though you wash yourself with lye and use much soap, the stain of your guilt is still before me, says the Lord God."[92] David implores God both to forgive his sins and wash away the stain of his sins.[93] We cannot appear before God with the stain of sin, for Scripture says Christ will present us "in splendor, without spot or wrinkle or any such thing, that she [the Church] might be holy and without blemish." (Eph 5:27).

To understand the temporal penalties from Original Sin, we go back to the Book of Genesis. When Adam and Eve disobeyed God's command in the Garden of Eden by listening to Satan and eating the forbidden fruit, God imposed upon them the penalty He had warned them about: "for in the day that you eat of it you shall die." (Gen 2:17). This meant both physical and spiritual death for them and their progeny. As Paul says in his Letter to the Romans, "Therefore as sin came into the world through one man and death through

92. Jer 2:22; cf. Jos 22:17.
93. Cf. Ps 51:1–2, 7, 9–10.

sin . . . so death spread to all men because all men sinned."
(5:12). Thus, death is not natural to man; it is a punishment
for sin, "because God did not make death." (Wis 1:13).

The penalty of death had two components: eternal and
temporal. The eternal punishment deprived Adam and Eve
(and all of us) of eternal life with God. Had Adam and Eve
persevered in their state of innocence and grace, God would
have translated them from their earthly paradise into His
heavenly paradise, which was represented in the Garden by
the "tree of life." (3:22). But because of their sin, God banished them from His eternal paradise where they would no
longer "live for ever."

The temporal punishment also had two components:
physical and spiritual. The physical component affected
Adam and Eve's bodies, which effects included suffering and
death. Scripture enumerates some others. For example, the
woman would be subject to weariness during pregnancy, to
pain during childbirth, and to her husband's will in obedience, even if it clashed with her own will.[94] The man would
have difficulty in his labors because God had cursed the earth
and caused it to bring forth thorns and thistles, making it
physically difficult for him to earn his daily bread (vv. 17–19).

In Genesis 3:6–19 we see that the spiritual component—
that is, the concupiscence—affected Adam and Eve's souls,
such that their flesh would be in conflict with their spirit.
Here too Scripture enumerates specific effects. For example, the woman would desire to rule over her husband out
of pride.[95] The man would be burdened by labor out of

---

94. Cf. Gen 3:16. This punishment did not concern the husband's headship over
the family, for he was the head of his wife and children even before the Fall
(see Eph 5:22–24; Col 3:18; Tit 2:5; and 1 Pet 3:1–2).

95. The Hebrew word for "desire" (*teshuqah*) can mean a desire to rule over
someone, and not a desire of affection.

weakness of spirit. In seeing each other naked, both of them would experience confusion from their disordered carnal appetites. They would also be burdened with the reminder of their impending death. These physical and spiritual punishments would affect mankind's very existence and its relationship with the God who created them.

Although these punishments were severe, God promised from the moment He imposed them to send a Savior to free men from the grip of Satan. In what is often called the Protoevangelium (which means "First Gospel"), God declares to the devil, "I will put enmity between you and the woman, and between your seed and her seed; he shall bruise your head, and you shall bruise his heel."[96] God would later reveal through His prophets that the "enmity" would be His only begotten Son, Jesus Christ, who would atone for the eternal penalty of sin, thereby restoring man to eternal life: "For God so loved the world that he gave his only Son, that whoever believes in him should not perish but have eternal life." (Jn 3:16).

God did send His Son to restore us to life everlasting. But it should be obvious to any Christian that Jesus didn't fully atone for the temporal punishments associated with Original Sin. After all, everyone experiences the effects of bodily weakness and spiritual concupiscence in their lives. It's a daily struggle. We feel aches and pains in our bodies. We often find physical labor tedious and tiresome. We feel our sensual appetites playing havoc with our reason. We are

---

96. Gen 3:15. The Fathers of the Church teach that the "enmity" (as well as the seed) is Christ and the "woman" is the Blessed Virgin Mary. In fact, the Hebrew in Genesis 3:15 demonstrates that it will be the woman—Mary—who will crush the head of the devil at the end of the world (this is because the singular pronoun *hu*, which is often translated as "he," relates back to the noun *ha-isha* which means "woman"). The Latin Vulgate also says "*ipsa conteret*" ("she shall bruise").

wounded with self-love and pride. We know something is not quite right inside of us. This is because our soul is at war with our flesh: "For the desires of the flesh are against the Spirit, and the desires of the Spirit are against the flesh; for these are opposed to each other, to prevent you from doing what you would." (Gal 5:17).

Scripture is clear that we have inherited the temporal effects of Original Sin. In his Letter to the Romans, Paul says, "For as by one man's disobedience many were made sinners, so by one man's obedience many will be made righteous." (Rom 5:19). The word for "made" (from the Greek, *kathistemi*) refers to making or changing a character or nature to make it other than it was before.[97] This means that God has *infused in our nature* the sin and concupiscence of Adam. David also says, "Behold, I was brought forth in iniquity, and in sin did my mother conceive me." (Ps 51:5). Although Christ has atoned for the eternal punishment of Adam's sin, He has allowed these temporal punishments to remain, for the reasons we saw above.

This reality supports the Catholic teaching on baptism and grace. As we will further discuss below, just as God infuses into our nature Adam's sin by generation, He infuses into our nature the grace of Jesus Christ by regeneration. (Cf. Tit 3:5). There is a correspondence between the actual change in our nature by sin (through natural birth) and the actual change in our nature by grace (through the supernatural rebirth of baptism). As Paul says, "where sin increased, grace abounded all the more." (Rom 5:20). This is why baptism is necessary for salvation. Jesus says, "He who believes and is baptized will be saved; but he who does not believe will be condemned." (Mk 16:16). The Apostle Peter also says that baptism "saves

---

97. Note similar usages in Heb 7:28; Jas 4:4; 2 Pet 1:8.

you" through the grace of Jesus Christ. (Cf. 1 Pet 3:21).

Because the soul is infused with grace, sin acts upon it like a stain, as Scripture teaches. We certainly understand how corporeal things are stained when they come into contact with certain other things. For example, a white cloth is stained when it comes into contact with mud. Even though the soul is spiritual and not corporeal, it can be stained as well. Why? Because the soul is illumined by the light of reason and the Divine light of God through grace. The effect of the remnants of sin is to cause a privation of this light of grace—a stain. Mortal sin expels sanctifying grace entirely from the soul and darkens it completely. This is why Scripture associates grace with light and sin with darkness.[98]

When a person repents of his sin and God forgives him, God restores his soul to the state of grace. This is part of the salvation process. However, this doesn't mean that the person is automatically restored to the position he was in before he sinned. If we understand sin to be an irrational movement toward a mutable good, only a contrary movement can restore the original balance. As we have seen, this contrary movement is analogous to making satisfaction for sin. For example, if someone moves away from God by committing the sin of gluttony, fasting would be a contrary movement (a self-imposed temporal punishment) that can make satisfaction for the sin. The sin (gluttony) transgressed the order of divine justice, and the contrary movement (fasting) restores the sinner to the equality of justice. Again, he who has overindulged his will must suffer something contrary to what he would wish in order to restore justice. If the sinner does not restore in this life the justice that God demands, he will do so in the next, which is purgatory.

---

98. Cf. Mt 6:23; Lk 1:79; Jn 1:5; 3:19; 8:12; 12:35, 46; Rom 2:19; 13:12; 1 Cor 4:5; 2 Cor 4:6; 6:14; Eph 5:8, 11; 1 Thess 5:4–5; 1 Pet 2:9; 1 Jn 1:5–6; 2:8–9, 11.

In his letter to the Romans, Paul explains the effects of concupiscence in his own body:

> I do not understand my own actions. For I do not do what I want, but I do the very thing I hate. Now if I do what I do not want, I agree that the law is good. So then it is no longer I that do it, but sin which dwells within me. For I know that nothing good dwells within me, that is, in my flesh. I can will what is right, but I cannot do it. For I do not do the good I want, but the evil I do not want is what I do. Now if I do what I do not want, it is no longer I that do it, but sin which dwells within me. (7:15–20).

Paul is describing the tension between the two faculties of the soul: The intellective and sensitive. The intellective faculty includes the reason and the will, while the sensitive includes the lower appetite or passions. As we have said when defining concupiscence, because of our wounded nature the lower appetite is inclined to sin (for example, gluttony, lust, anger, sloth). If the intellective lacks due rule over the sensitive, the will produces the act of sin. Because all the soul's powers are rooted in the one essence of the soul, when one power intends to act (lower), another power is necessarily weakened or even impeded (higher). This is why the reason and will give way to sin. The intellective is overpowered by the sensitive.

Hence, sin originates within the soul, and it is chiefly in the will.[99] This is why Paul exhorts us to cleanse ourselves from "defilement of spirit" in order to achieve holiness.[100]

---

99. Because God loves all things He has created (Wis 11:24) but hates sin (Wis 14:9) demonstrates that God is not the cause or author of sin.
100. Cf. 2 Cor 7:1.

Jesus says, "But what comes out of the mouth proceeds from the heart, and this defiles a man. For out of the heart come evil thoughts, murder, adultery, fornication, theft, false witness, slander. These are what defile a man."[101] Jesus also says, "Blessed are the pure in heart, for they shall see God." (Mt 5:8). James further says, "each person is tempted when he is lured and enticed by his own desire. Then desire when it has conceived gives birth to sin; and sin when it is full-grown brings forth death." (1:14–15).

Because sin originates in the soul, the soul must be purified of its inclinations to sin before entering the heavenly beatitude. As we have stated, these inclinations are not only from the concupiscence we have inherited from Adam, but are also produced in the soul through habitual actual sin. Even when a sin is forgiven, the sinful disposition caused by preceding acts can remain. Concupiscence, remnants of sin, and debts of temporal punishment all defile a man's soul, making purification necessary. These are objective conditions in the eyes of Almighty God; death doesn't change the state of the soul. If the soul is in grace but not completely freed from these impurities, God will complete the purification in purgatory.

Discipline Versus Punishment

In light of the clear teachings of Scripture, most Protestants acknowledge that God imposes temporal penalties upon us for our actual sins. Many also acknowledge that these temporal penalties include the soul's disordered inclinations resulting from Original Sin and the remnants of sin. However, in an effort to deny purgatory, Protestants contend that God

---

101. Mt 15:18–19; see also Mk 7:21.

doesn't impose these punishments on us as a satisfaction for sin, but as a "discipline" for saved Christians to increase their sanctification. If making satisfaction is unnecessary, then purgatory is unnecessary. Thus, Protestants view temporal penalties not as a means of retribution, but sanctification only. There are several problems with this position.

The first and most obvious problem with this argument is that it is an arbitrary and semantic distinction. There is no difference between the terms "discipline" and "punishment," either in their everyday usage or the way in which they are used in Scripture. When a father punishes a son, he disciplines him. He brings him back to the order of justice by imposing on him a "discipline" against his will. This discipline introduces what we have referred to as a "contrary movement" which restores the scales of equity. This is the retributive purpose for temporal punishment.

The Book of Proverbs equates "discipline" with "punishment" when it says, "Do not withhold discipline from a child; if you beat him with a rod, he will not die." (23:13). Paul also uses "discipline" and "punishment" as synonyms when he says, "do not regard lightly the discipline of the Lord, nor lose courage when you are punished by him." (Heb 12:5). In fact, Scripture also uses "discipline" to describe how God tests departed souls in the fire of His divine justice "like gold in the furnace"—a clear reference to purgatory.[102]

Secondly, the examples of temporal punishment in Scripture reveal that they were not primarily to sanctify the Elect. They instead reveal an emphasis on the exacting nature of God's punitive justice. For example, when God punishes the Israelites by preventing them from seeing the Promised Land, Scripture indicates that most of them were

---

102. Cf. Wis 3:1–7.

hard-hearted unbelievers on the road to damnation.[103]

Paul reveals that these Jews were "natural branches broken off from the root because of their unbelief."[104] In fact, notwithstanding God's temporal punishment for their idolatry and sexual immorality at Sinai, the Jews would later fall into the same sins at Beth-peor! (Cf. Num 25:1–5). For their wickedness, God sends them a plague that kills twenty-four thousand. Hence, far from sanctifying the Israelites, God's temporal punishment at Sinai would be a portend of their eternal punishment at Peor.[105]

We also see how God imposes temporal penalties of weakness and illness on the members of the Corinthian church. The Corinthians had been causing drunken disturbances before celebrating the Lord's Supper.[106] After Paul warns them that abusing the Eucharist results in eternal judgment, he says, "That is why many of you are weak and ill, and some have died." (1 Cor 11:30). Thus, Paul suggests that the temporal penalties of sickness, far from sanctifying the Corinthians, foreshadowed the eternal damnation of some of them. Paul's repeated warnings about falling away from the faith also demonstrate that he is not exhorting "saved Christians to grow in holiness," but questioning whether they will be saved at all.[107]

Thirdly, if temporal penalties dealt with God's "sanctifying

---

103. Cf. Isa 10:22; Mic 2:12; Rom 9:25; 11:5, 14.

104. Cf. Rom 11:17–23. The root (Greek, *rhiza*) refers to Jesus Christ and not "Israel" as some Jewish apologists contend (see Jn 15:6; Rom 15:12; Rev 5:5).

105. This does not mean temporal punishments are a sign of future eternal punishment. To the contrary, we should view temporal punishments as a blessing from God, who desires our purification in this life rather than in the next. It is only when man fails to repent of his mortal sins that he incurs eternal punishment.

106. Cf. 1 Cor 11:18–21.

107. Cf. 1 Cor 3:17; 4:5; 6:8–9; 9:27–10:6, 11–12; 15:1–2; 2 Cor 5:20–6:2; 11:3; 12:21–13:5.

discipline" but not His desire to restore the equality of justice, we would not expect to see Scripture connect "discipline" with "salvation." That is because God determines
salvation or damnation under the auspices of His justice,
whereas the Protestant notion of "discipline" is reserved for
those who are already saved.

However, in his Epistle to the Hebrews, Paul says that
"discipline" produces "holiness," which is necessary for salvation.[108] While Protestants would like to define "discipline"
in Hebrews as the means of sanctification for already-saved
Christians, Hebrews 12:10 puts "discipline" in a salvific context.[109] The Book of Proverbs also says, in the context of
damnation, "He dies for lack of discipline, and because of
his great folly he is lost."[110]

In his letter to the Romans, we saw how Paul makes
our salvation contingent upon our suffering when he says
we are fellow heirs with Christ, "provided we suffer with
him in order that we may also be glorified with him."
(Rom 8:17). The Greek for "in order" (*eiper*) is a conditional
participle, which renders Paul's glorification contingent
upon his sufferings.

In his Letter to the Philippians, Paul says, "that I may
know him and the power of his resurrection, and may share
his sufferings, becoming like him in his death, that if possible I may attain the resurrection from the dead." (3:10–11).
The Greek for "if possible" (*ei pos*) is a conditional phrase

---

108. 12:10. Cf. Heb 12:14. Moreover, it is clear that Paul doesn't view the
    Hebrews' salvation as guaranteed as almost fifty percent of the book is
    devoted to warning them that they can fall from their salvation.
109. 12:10. The Greek supports this conclusion. The word for discipline (from
    the Greek, *paideia*) in verses 5–7 and 9 (regarding disciplining sons) is the
    same word Paul uses in verse 10 (regarding discipline that produces the
    holiness needed for salvation).
110. 5:23. See also Prov 15:10; 19:18; Jer 7:28.

which means that Paul believes his suffering is a condition for salvation, not just a means for greater sanctity. Moreover, Paul's statement reveals that he doesn't view his salvation as guaranteed. If the Apostle Paul believed his salvation wasn't a certainty, how can any Christian not offend God by presuming his own salvation?

In his First Letter to the Corinthians, Paul reveals his own struggles with the flesh and says, "but I pommel my body and subdue it, lest after preaching to others I myself should be disqualified." (1 Cor 9:27). Again, Paul believes that his sufferings lead to salvation, and his failure to suffer with Christ leads to damnation. The Greek word for "disqualified" (*adokimos*) literally means "reprobate," or one who is to be condemned to hell. Paul uses the word five other times in the New Testament, and every time it refers to the eternally condemned.

For example, Paul uses *adokimos* to describe idolaters and sodomites,[111] evildoers,[112] rebels against God-given authority,[113] corrupted unbelievers,[114] and the accursed who are to burn in hell.[115] In each case, Paul is describing people who God has allowed to perish in hell, not those whom He is sanctifying for heaven. Even though Paul was converted directly by Jesus Christ and was an instrument of God's revelation, he still believed his damnation was a possibility if he fell from grace. Contrary to what many Protestants believe, Scripture is replete with passages revealing that currently "saved" Christians can lose their salvation through sin.[116]

---

111. Rom 1:28.
112. 2 Cor 13:5–7.
113. 2 Tim 3:8.
114. Tit 1:15–16.
115. Heb 6:8.
116. Cf. Mt 7:21–23; 10:22, 28, 33; 24:12–13; Mk 13:22; Lk 8:13; Jn 12:47–48; 15:6; Acts 13:43, 46; 20:29–30; Rom 2:6; 11:20–22; 1 Cor 4:5; 10:11–12;

This also means that Scripture does not distinguish between sanctification and salvation.[117] To the contrary, Scripture uses these two words to describe the same thing: a soul in a state of grace. For example, in his first letter to the Thessalonians, Paul says, "For this is the will of God, your sanctification: that you abstain from immorality . . . not in the passion of lust like heathen who do not know God . . . because the Lord is an avenger in all these things." (4:3–6). If committing these mortal sins (immorality, lust) leads to damnation, then avoiding these sins leads to salvation. Hence, Paul uses sanctification as a synonym for salvation.[118]

The point is this: If the Protestant's premise about the nature of suffering in this life is wrong, then his conclusion that there is no suffering in the next life is wrong as well. If the Protestant mischaracterizes the purpose of earthly suffering, he has no basis to deny the reality of purgatorial suffering. If suffering produces holiness, which is necessary for heaven as Scripture teaches, then suffering cannot be limited to non-salvific sanctification or the accrual of heavenly rewards. As Scripture teaches, suffering—whether it's called "chastisement," "discipline," or "punishment"—is the vehicle that restores man to the equality of God's justice,

---

15:1–2; 2 Cor 5:20–6:2; 11:3; 12:21–13:5; Eph 5:5–6; Col 1:21–23; 1 Thess 4:1–8; 2 Thess 2:13–15; 1Tim 4:1; 5:15; 6:10; 2 Tim 1:15; 2:12, 17; 4:10, 16; Heb 2:1; 3:1, 6, 12–14; 4:1, 11–14; 6:4–6, 11–12; 10:26–27, 35–38; 12:1–3, 14–17, 25, 29; Jas 1:21–22; 1 Pet 4:18; 5:8; 2 Pet 1:9; 2:20–22; 3:14–17; 1 Jn 2:24–26, 28; 2 Jn 8; Rev 2:5, 10, 16, 23, 26; 3:3, 11, 16, 21; 16:15.

117. If "sanctification" simply referred to a saved person's accrual of rewards, one would expect the word "sanctification" to chronologically follow Scripture's use of "salvation" or "justification." Instead, the only time a Scripture verse mentions justification/salvation along with sanctification, the word "sanctification" precedes "justification." See 1 Cor 6:11.

118. Paul does the same thing in Acts 20:32, Rom 6:22, 1 Cor 1:30 and 2 Thess 2:13. Paul also says one can fall from sanctification (salvation) in Heb 10:29.

appeases God's anger, and moves man to salvation through repentance.

Grace and the Salvation Process

As we have alluded to, most Protestants reject the doctrine of purgatory because of a faulty understanding of how God justifies (saves) sinners. Both Catholics and Protestants agree that justification is the process whereby man, moved by God's grace, accepts God's forgiveness and righteousness. Being in a state of justification means we are in a right relationship with God, making us children of God and heirs of heaven. Hence, Catholics and Protestants agree that justification and salvation are the same thing. The difference, however, between Catholic and Protestant theology is how a person becomes justified (saved). This difference affects not only how one views the status of the sinner in this life, but also in the afterlife (which means it affects one's view of purgatory).

As we learned in the Preface, the doctrine of purgatory invokes a broad range of theological territory. If one theological presupposition is wrong, the entire theology unravels. False premises lead to false conclusions. We will close this chapter by examining in more detail the most common Protestant rebuttal to purgatory.[119] Although a thorough examination is beyond the scope of this book, addressing the basic premises of the Protestant position will allow us to see the errors in their rejection of purgatory and the truth of the Catholic, biblical position.

---

119. It must be noted that there are many different views within Protestantism regarding how God saves man. We have chosen to focus on "faith alone" and "imputed righteousness" because they are the most common positions Protestants use to deny the Catholic doctrine of purgatory.

"Faith Alone" and "Imputed Righteousness"

We have already mentioned how many Protestants view Christ's atonement as a legal transaction. We will now explore this concept in greater depth, and we will begin our analysis with an irony: Protestants reject purgatory, in part, based on a Scripture verse in Revelation that Catholics use in support of purgatory. We have already seen this verse: "But nothing unclean shall enter it, nor any one who practices abomination or falsehood, but only those who are written in the Lamb's book of life." (21:27).

Because we are sinners and nothing unclean can enter heaven, the Protestant concludes that we can never possess heaven-worthy righteousness on our own. Because God demands perfect righteousness and we are imperfect, the righteousness required for heaven must come from outside of us. Therefore, the Protestant concludes, to make us worthy of heaven God credits us with Christ's righteousness—the righteousness that Christ displayed during His Passion. According to this view, the "crediting" of Christ's righteousness to the sinner's account is not unlike an accountant making a credit entry on his books. Christ's sacrificial death is viewed as a legal or forensic transaction, and not a personal propitiation.

To receive the crediting (or imputing) of Christ's righteousness, the Protestant says that the sinner simply needs to believe that Jesus died for his sins. Since there is no work a sinner can do to make himself righteous, the sinner accepts the righteousness of Christ's atoning work by that faith alone. After this solitary profession of faith in Jesus Christ, God credits the sinner's ledger and legally declares him to be justified (saved). Upon receiving his justification, the now-saved sinner transitions into a new phase of Christian life called sanctification. In this phase, the sinner lives a life of prayer, penance, and good works, a life that demonstrates his once-for-all justification and builds up his rewards in heaven. Hence, in Protestant theology, justification (salvation) is a one-time event, and sanctification is the ongoing process that follows justification.

In the state of justification, the Protestant contends that when God evaluates our lives, He sees only Christ's righteousness (which has been credited), and not our sinfulness (which has been covered). It follows that, when we die, being "covered" with Christ's righteousness makes us automatically pure in God's sight and worthy of the Beatific Vision. God sees no "stain of sin" or "debt of punishment," but only the righteousness of Christ, which He credited to us at our justification. Thus, at death, God needs only to determine our level of rewards for the deeds we have accomplished during the sanctification phase. This Protestant construct eliminates any need for purgatory.

At first blush, this theory seems reasonable. After all, when we look critically at ourselves, we cannot imagine being sufficiently righteous to merit heaven. If God truly judges every thought, word, and deed, how could we possibly be found worthy of being admitted into God's dwelling place? Isn't it easier to let Christ be our substitute? Isn't it easier to let "faith alone" be our judge; for the deeds we have done in this life to determine only the reward we will receive in heaven, and not our eternal salvation or damnation? While this position seems sensible, there is a reason why no Christian ever heard of it until the Protestant revolt in the sixteenth century.[120]

---

120. The theory of imputed righteousness was first introduced into Christian thought by Martin Luther during the Reformation, 1,500 years after Christ ascended into heaven. Luther analogized his novel doctrine to snow covering a dunghill (which he witnessed on the hillsides in Germany). The

First, when we read Revelation 21:27, there is nothing about "imputed righteousness" in the verse. The Apostle John equates being "unclean" with those who practice "abomination or falsehood" (v. 27), not with those who haven't been appropriated Christ's righteousness by their faith. In the same chapter, John excludes from heaven "murderers, fornicators, sorcerers, idolaters, and all liars" (v. 8).[121] In other words, John is revealing that one is "unclean" based upon what he does during his life, not upon whether he has received a legal imputation of Christ's righteousness. God judges what the person actually is, not what he appears to be when "covered" by the righteousness of Christ.

Secondly, Catholics agree with Protestants that there is nothing we can do by our own actions to deserve eternal life. We cannot rid ourselves of the title "unclean" by our own efforts. Because of our sinfulness, neither our faith nor our works can be sufficiently pleasing to God to merit heaven. While this might surprise many Protestants, the Catholic Council of Trent, the same council that defined purgatory, dogmatically declared: "If anyone says that man can be justified before God by his own works, whether done by his own natural powers or through the teaching of the law, without divine grace through Jesus Christ, let him be anathema."[122]

This is precisely where the Protestant position breaks down. Why?

Because, on the one hand, it requires the sinner to have faith to merit Christ's imputed righteousness, and on the

---

Catholic view is that the snow does not cover, but actually sinks into the soil, to produce "flowers" and "fruits" that are pleasing to God.

121. See also 22:11, 15 where John continues the theme of what people have actually done during their lives, not whether their faith made them worthy of the imputed righteousness of Christ.

122. Council of Trent, Session 6, Canon 1, *Decrees on Justification* (January 13, 1547).

other hand, it says that there is nothing the sinner can do to please God. Which is it, faith or nothing? This is a blatant inconsistency in the Protestant position. If our works cannot please God, then our faith cannot please God either. If our works are imperfect because of sin and, thus, cannot merit heaven, then our faith is imperfect as well. If our faith is imperfect, then that faith cannot merit a crediting of Christ's righteousness, or any consideration from God at all. How do we reconcile this contradiction? The Scriptures and the Church have the answer, and the answer is grace.

When we are born into the world, because of the sin of Adam we lack a gracious relationship with God. That is, we lack grace, which is an unmerited sharing in the life of God. As we have seen, on account of Original Sin, we have inherited both the eternal punishment for Adam's sin (hell), as well as the temporal penalties for his sin, which are both physical (weakness, death) and spiritual (concupiscence). As Paul says, we are born under the condemnation "of the law."[123] In this state of condemnation, there is absolutely nothing we can do, whether it be faith or works, to merit anything from God.

When we are "born again" in baptism, God infuses sanctifying grace into our souls.[124] This grace simultaneously justifies and sanctifies us, thereby restoring us to a gracious relationship with God. Paul says we are "justified by his grace" through the "washing of regeneration" which God

---

123. Rom 4:15; Gal 3:10.
124. Note that God always takes the first step by moving man to baptism through what is called actual or prevenient grace. In this first step, man is still under God's condemnation and does not have the theological virtue of faith. It is only through baptism that man first receives sanctifying grace and the virtues of faith, hope and charity. A man's will cannot move toward God unless God, the Prime Mover, moves it (see, for example, Ps 79:4, 8, 20; 84:5; Jer 31:18; Lam 5:21).

"pours out upon us." [125] Paul also tells the Corinthians the salvific effects of their baptism when he says, "you were washed, you were sanctified, you were justified in the name of the Lord Jesus Christ and in the Spirit of our God." [126] Paul likely uses the word "wash" for baptism because he heard the same terminology used at his own baptism, when Ananias told Paul, "Rise and be baptized, and wash away your sins." [127]

Through the infusion of grace at baptism, God washes away Original Sin and the eternal penalty of sin by virtue of the merits of Jesus Christ (although God, as we have seen, allows the temporal penalties to remain). Baptism also gives us the theological virtues of "faith," "hope," and "charity," which God has "poured into our hearts through the Holy Spirit who has been given to us." [128] Baptism cleanses the interior of the person because it makes "our hearts sprinkled clean from an evil conscience and our bodies washed with pure water." (Heb 10:22). This is why Peter preached, "Repent, and be baptized every one of you in the name of Jesus Christ for the forgiveness of your sins." (Acts 2:38).

In this state of grace, which commences at baptism, God no longer deals with us as sons of Adam, but as His sons through Jesus Christ. Since we are His sons, God can be pleased with our faith and works because that is how a Father interacts with His children. [129] Scripture is replete

---

125. Cf. Tit 3:5–7.
126. 1 Cor 6:11. Notice that "sanctification" and "justification" (two aorist verbs) happen at the same time, and that "sanctification" chronologically precedes "justification" in the verse.
127. Acts 22:16. The word for "wash away" (Greek, *apolouo*) is used in both Acts 22:16 and 1 Cor 6:11, the only two times it is used in the New Testament.
128. Cf. Rom 5:1–5.
129. It is important to note that God moves man by His grace to do good, for man can do nothing without God (Jn 15:5). Thus, when man does penance to make satisfaction for his sins, it is God's grace that produces the effect

with verses revealing how we are able to "please" God by our efforts when in a state of grace.[130] Paul says, "So whether we are at home or away, we make it our aim to please him." (2 Cor 5:9) and that we must "lead a life worthy of the Lord, fully pleasing to him" (Col 1:10). Paul further says, "we speak not to please men, but to please God who tests our hearts." (1 Thess 2:4). John also says, "We receive from him whatever we ask because we keep his commandments and do what pleases him." (1 Jn 3:22).

As we persevere in the virtues of faith, hope, and charity, which we received in baptism, God increases the measure of sanctifying grace in our souls. The process of infusion is ongoing: the more grace we receive from God, the more pleasing we are to Him. Grace strengthens our power to do God's will and increases our merit and favor before Him. Hence, grace is not only the life of God within us, but a "divine substance" that God infuses into the soul. Grace has real existence, which is why it is sometimes called "ontic" grace (related to the word "ontology" which is the study of being or existence). The scriptures reveal many examples where grace is described in terms of a measurable quantity.[131]

We recall Paul's statement in Romans 5:19: "For as by one man's disobedience many were made sinners, so by one man's obedience many will be made righteous."[132] Just as we

---

in man. While man has freewill, God's grace moves man "both to will and to work for his good pleasure" (Phil 2:13). As Augustine says, when God accepts our good works, He is simply crowning His own gifts.

130. Cf. Rom 8:8; 1 Cor 7:32; Col 3:20; 4:1; Heb 11:6.

131. Cf. Acts 4:23; Rom 12:6; Eph 4:7; Jas 4:6; 1 Pet 4:10; 2 Pet 1:2.

132. The word "righteous" in Romans 5:19 (Greek, *díkaios*) is the same word Scripture applies to many holy people, such as Joseph (Mt 1:19), John the Baptist (Mk 6:20), Zechariah and Elizabeth (Lk 1:6), Simeon (Lk 2:25), Joseph of Arimathea (Lk 23:50) and Lot (2 Pet 2:7).

were made sinners by the infusion of Original Sin (through the natural generation of conception), we are also made righteous by the infusion of grace (through the supernatural regeneration of baptism). Based on the comparative clauses of Romans 5:19, we must conclude that there is an objective change in our nature if we are to maintain exegetical equilibrium in the verse. If we truly have been infected with Original Sin (and we see that we are by the concupiscence of the soul), then we truly are made righteous by grace through Jesus Christ.

Paul also says, "If, because of one man's trespass, death reigned through that one man, much more will those who receive the abundance of grace and the free gift of righteousness reign in life through the one man Jesus Christ." (Rom 5:17). Again, Paul says that the remedy for Original Sin is to receive grace and righteousness through Christ, not merely to be covered by it through some legal imputation. What we receive, we possess. God gives this grace to us in baptism, and we must cooperate with this grace to obtain "acquittal and life for all men" (v. 18). This acquittal refers to both the eternal and temporal punishments that we have inherited from "the one man's trespass" (vv. 17–18).

"It Was Credited to Him as Righteousness"

Let's recall why we began this discussion. If God sees only the righteousness of Christ when he judges the sinner upon his death, then, as we have stated, purgatory would be unnecessary. However, if God doesn't merely "cover" the person with Christ's righteousness, then the Protestant cannot object to the Catholic doctrine on those grounds. Further, if God doesn't see Christ's alien righteousness when He judges the sinner, then God must evaluate the sinner's own righteousness, for nothing unclean shall enter heaven. Since most of us do not achieve the perfect righteousness God demands for heaven—even when faithfully living the life of grace—well, that's where purgatory comes in.

So how do Protestants attempt to support the theory of "imputed righteousness" by "faith alone"? They attempt to demonstrate it primarily from the biblical account of Abraham. In the book of Genesis, we learn that God establishes a covenant with Abraham and his descendants by promising to give them land and prosperity.[133] Because Abraham and his wife Sara are elderly and childless, Abraham laments to God that he has no natural descendants and that his servant Eliezer will have to be his heir. God responds by revealing to Abraham, "This man shall not be your heir; your own son shall be your heir." (Gen 15:4).

Notwithstanding the perceived improbability of Abraham and Sara conceiving a child, Scripture says about Abraham: "And he believed the Lord; and he reckoned [credited] it to him as righteousness." (Gen 15:6). Paul confirms in his Letter to the Romans that Abraham was justified at this moment in time when he writes, "For if Abraham was justified by works, he has something to boast about, but not before God. For what does the scripture say? 'Abraham believed God, and it was reckoned to him as righteousness.' Now to one who works, his wages are not reckoned as a gift

---

133. There is a material and spiritual component to the covenant. Materially, God promises Abraham's descendants a physical dwelling place on earth (Gen 15:18–21). God fulfills this promise in Jos 21:43; Neh 9:7; and 1 Kg 8:5, which means today's Jews have no divine right to more land in Israel (thus refuting a movement called "Zionism"). Spiritually, God promises Abraham and his descendants a spiritual dwelling place in heaven (Gen 13:15; 17:7–8; 22:17–18; Heb 11:10, 16), and He fulfills this promise through the New Covenant, which is why Abraham is called the father of Christians (Rom 4:16; Gal 3:7, 16, 29).

but as his due."[134] Does this account support the doctrine of "imputed righteousness"? Let us see what the scriptures say. Paul does not say Abraham was justified by "faith alone." We also note that Scripture never says a man is justified by "faith alone." In fact, the only time the phrase "faith alone" is used in Scripture is in the Epistle of James, when James declares that "man is justified by works and not by faith alone." (Jas 2:24). Thus, Scripture teaches that faith, by itself, is insufficient to save the sinner, and that works must be added to faith. Scripture also teaches that we need a certain kind of faith to receive salvation, and that is a faith which is accompanied by obedience,[135] love,[136] and repentance.[137] For example, Paul refers to "the obedience of faith," requires a "faith working through love," and exhorts us to have "repentance to God and of faith in our Lord Jesus Christ."[138]

Furthermore, when Paul refers to "works" in Romans 4:2, he is referring to works that attempt to obligate God, and thus are performed outside of His grace.[139] That is why Paul connects "works" with "wages" (v. 4). He is warning the Romans not to treat God like an employer who owes them, but like a Father who loves them. An employee does not need to have faith in an employer, for the law

---

134. Rom 4:2–4. See also Gal 3:6; Jas 2:23. Catholics and Protestants agree that God saved people by the grace of the New Covenant even before the coming of Christ because God's eternal decree made Christ's sacrifice—the event that provided grace to mankind—an event that was certain to occur (Acts 2:23; see also 1 Pet 1:20).

135. Cf., Rom 6:16–17; 15:18; 16:26; 2 Cor 9:13; Heb 5:9.

136. Cf. Eph 6:23; Col 1:14; 1 Thess 1:3; 3:6; 5:8; 1Tim 1:14; 2 Tim 1:13; 3:10; Tit 2:2; Philm 5; Gal 5:6.

137. Cf. Mt 3:2; 4:17; Mk 1:15; 6:12; Lk 13:3, 5; Acts 2:38; 3:19; 8:22; 17:30, et al.

138. Rom 16:26; Gal 5:6; Acts 20:21.

139. Scripture distinguishes between faith that is exhibited in a state of grace (Jas 2:1, 8, 22) and faith that is outside of God's grace (Jas 2:14, 17, 19, 26), as well as works performed in grace (Jas 2:21–25) and works done outside of grace (Rom 4:4; 6:14, 23; 11:6; Eph 2;8–9).

obligates the employer to pay for services rendered.

However, God is not obligated to pay His creatures for their work because, as we have seen Paul say, "who has given a gift to him that he might be repaid?" (Rom 11:35). This is why Paul tells us that "the wages of sin is death." (Rom 6:23). That being said, Paul reveals to the Romans that now, as baptized Christians, they have a special relationship with God based on grace, not law.[140] In this new relationship, God will reward them for their works if they have faith in Him as their Father. This is because a good father rewards His children out of love, not legal obligation. (Cf. Heb 6:10; 11:6).

Finally, and perhaps most fundamentally, the Protestant assumes that what God "credits" to Abraham He doesn't actually see in Abraham. In other words, God declares that Abraham has changed but he hasn't really changed. To use the accounting analogy, the Protestant essentially argues that God makes a phony credit entry on the books. The problem with this position is obvious: it infringes upon the integrity and holiness of God who cannot lie or deceive us. (Cf. Tit 1:2; Heb 6:18). If a criminal judge doesn't pretend about the actual status of a defendant, why would the Supreme Judge pretend about the actual status of a sinner?

The original biblical language also assists us in this analysis. The Greek word for "credited" is *logizomai*. This word is used forty times in the New Testament and has various shades of meaning including "accepted," "considered," "counted," and "reckoned."[141] Whenever the word is applied to a person, it

---

140. Cf. Rom 4:16; 6:14; 11:6. As a subsidiary point, when Paul refers to "works" done under the auspices of obligation and not grace, he often means works done under the obsolete Mosaic law (cf. Rom 2:14; 3:20, 28; 4:13; 7:4–7; 9:32; Acts 13:38; Gal 2:16; 3:17; Phil 3:9).

141. Mk 15:28; Lk 22:37; Acts 19:27; Rom 2:3; 3:28; 4:3–6, 8–11, 22–24; 6:11; 8:18, 36; 9:8; 14:14; 1 Cor 4:1; 13:5, 11; 2 Cor 3:5; 5:19; 10:2, 7, 11; 11:5; 12:6; Gal 3:6; Phil 3:13; 4:8; 2 Tim 4:16; Heb 11:19; Jas 2:23; 1 Pet 5:12.

almost invariably refers to an observation of something that actually exists in or about the person. It never refers to what a person is lacking.

When Scripture says God was not "counting [*logizomai*] their trespasses against them," they really had trespasses that God was willing to forgive. (Cf. 2 Cor 5:19). When Scripture says Abraham "considered [*logizomai*] that God was able to raise men even from the dead," Abraham really believed God could do it. (Cf. Heb 11:19). This means that when God "credited" [*logizomai*] Abraham with righteousness, Abraham really was righteous, and God was simply affirming what He saw in Abraham. If God, then, is judging Abraham's own righteousness, the Protestant doctrine of "imputed righteousness" is erroneous.

Some Protestants argue that God imputes Christ's righteousness to us because God imputes our sins to Christ on the Cross. Protestants may get this interpretation from Paul's statement to the Corinthians that God "made him to be sin who knew no sin, so that in him we might become the righteousness of God." (2 Cor 5:21). This interpretation is a grave error. First, the Church and all of the early Fathers always interpreted Paul's statement to mean that Christ was made a propitiatory offering for sin, but did not become sin itself. The Protestant interpretation is heretical because the divine Person of Jesus Christ could never assume anything sinful or evil. As Paul says, "what fellowship has light with darkness? What accord has Christ with Belial?" (2 Cor 6:14–15).

Note also that Scripture never uses *logizomai* in reference to Christ, but to man only. This means that the Protestant interpretation is not supported by Scripture. Just because Romans 5:19 teaches that we were infused with Adam's sin does not mean that Christ was infused with our sin. We were infused with Adam's sin because of Adam's disobedience, and we are freed of Adam's sin because of Christ's obedience, that is, Christ's freewill offering of Himself for our sins. This is how we become (not how we are imputed with) the "righteousness of God." (2 Cor 5:21).

Abraham's Justification

Paul's detailed account of Abraham's justification in his letters to the Romans and Hebrews further demonstrates the Catholic position: justification is an ongoing process of living out God's grace, not a one-time event of receiving Christ's alien righteousness. In describing Abraham's justification, Paul never speaks about a righteousness that is extrinsic to Abraham. Instead, Paul speaks very forcefully about Abraham's own intrinsic righteousness, which he developed over the course of his life as God tested him with severe trials, to which Abraham responded with the help of God's grace.

For example, Paul recalls how in Genesis 12 Abraham received the grace of salvation when he embarked on his journey to the Promised Land, looking for the city "whose builder and maker is God."[142] Even though in Genesis 12 Abraham had salvific and justifying faith, Paul says that Abraham was also "credited with righteousness" in Genesis 15:6, twenty-five years later, when he "believed against hope" that God would make him a father of many nations.[143] Paul

---

142. Heb 11:8–10,16; Gal 3:8–9; Gen 12:1–3.
143. V. 19. Cf. Rom 4:3; Gen 15:6; Rom 4:18. Most Protestants argue that Abraham was first justified in Genesis 15:6. But Heb 11:8 is clear that Abraham was justified in Genesis 12:1–3, for he had the same justifying "faith" as Abel, Enoch, Noah, Isaac, Jacob, Joseph, Moses, Rahab, and other Old Testament saints (see Heb 11:4–39). This proves that Gen 15:6, like Gen 12 and Gen 22, is an example of Abraham's progressive justification.

says, "He did not weaken in faith" when God promised him a son in his elder years, even though his body "was as good as dead because he was about a hundred years old, or when he considered the barrenness of Sarah's womb."[144]

Paul further recalls Abraham's most severe test, years later, in Genesis 22, where God asks Abraham to slay Isaac his son, for he believed "that God was able to raise men even from the dead."[145] James says Abraham was "credited with righteousness" at this moment as well, in Genesis 22, just as he was twenty-five years earlier in Genesis 15:6.[146] This, again, proves that Scripture teaches justification is a progressive development, not a static event. God continues to "credit" us with righteousness as we continue to do righteous deeds by the power of His grace. After Paul recounts all of these events in Abraham's life, he concludes by saying, "That is why his faith was 'reckoned to him as righteousness.'" (Rom 4:22).

The story of Abraham shows us that salvation is a process of growing in grace and righteousness, not a one-time event of receiving it by legal declaration. God works with us through His grace and continues to draw out faith, hope, and charity over our lifetime through trials and tests. This He does to obtain satisfaction for our sin, purify our hearts, and prepare our soul for heaven because "nothing unclean shall enter it." When we please God by living holy lives in

---

144. Romans 4:18–21. See also Heb 11:11.
145. Heb 11:19. God may have made Abraham prove he would slay his son as a temporal punishment for momentarily disbelieving that God could give him a natural heir in his and Sara's old age. See Gen 17:17 where Abraham laughed at God for making such a promise. Imposing the punishment of killing his son was a movement contrary to Abraham's intense desire to have a son, restoring to Abraham to the equality of justice for have disbelieved that God could give him a son.
146. Cf. Jas 2:21–23; Rom 4:3; Gen 22:17.

grace, we "become the righteousness of God." (2 Cor 5:21). As the Psalmist says, "The Lord rewarded me according to my righteousness."[147] Just as we share in Christ's righteousness by grace, we also "share his holiness." (Heb 12:10). This is why the Apostle John can say, "He who does right is righteous, as he is righteous."[148]

Thus, when God "credits" Abraham and anyone else with righteousness, it means that God looks at our very being and sees the internal quality of our own righteousness within us. God peers into the soul of man to evaluate his level of perfection and how he has used, or abused, grace. As Scripture teaches, God "works with us" by His grace to help us achieve the holiness necessary for heaven, and this is a life-long process.[149] If we persevere in grace to the end of our lives as Abraham did, we will receive the reward of salvation.[150] As Peter says, we will confirm our "call and election."[151] This is why Paul tells us that we must "follow the example of the faith" of Abraham. (Rom 4:12). This is the perfection that God demands of us to merit eternal life.

How does this relate to purgatory? Just as God peers into

---

147. Ps 18:20, 24.

148. 1 Jn 3:7. Note that when Paul says, "None is righteous, no, not one" (Rom 3:10; Ps 14:3; 53:3), he is referring to those who are still under the condemnation of the law, and not in grace (see also Tit 3:5–7). This is why Paul thereafter explains that one is not justified by the law of Moses but by the grace of Christ (Rom 3:19–26).

149. Cf. Mk 16:20; Rom 8:28; 1 Cor 3:9 and 2 Cor 6:1 for examples of how God "works" with us through the operation of grace. This doesn't mean the efficacy of God's grace is determined by man. Rather, God determines the efficacy of grace according to His eternal decrees. If God efficaciously wills man to attain to grace, then the grace will infallibly "work" in man by causing him to freely choose the good.

150. Cf. Heb 11:10,13,16.

151. 2 Pet 1:10. Even though God unconditionally wills the salvation of His elect and He always accomplishes His will, He gives all men sufficient grace to be saved. This is one of the most profound mysteries of the Faith.

our souls during life, He judges the condition of the soul at death. As He granted grace to the worthy soul during life, so He grants glory to that worthy soul at death. The presence or absence of grace in the soul at death determines our destination after death. If we die with sanctifying grace in our souls, we go to heaven. If we die in a state of grace but our soul is stained (with venial sin or the debt of punishment), we go to purgatory before heaven. Purgatory is an objective necessity because the soul's condition at death is an objective reality—and this is what God looks at when He judges us.

David's Justification

The story of David teaches us the same thing about justification, but with additional insights. Many years before David commits the mortal sins of adultery and murder, God describes David as "a man after my heart."[152] No one else in Scripture is described in this lofty way. David had "the Spirit of the Lord," wrote inspired Scripture (the Psalms), and enjoyed a very intimate relationship with God.[153] In a word, David was as "saved" as they come. Many Protestants believe that no one with such an incredible relationship with God could possibly fall from grace. But David did.

After David commits his sins of adultery and murder, he confesses them to God and God forgives him. In thanksgiving to God, David writes Psalms 32 and 51 about God's merciful forgiveness. In his letter to the Romans, Paul refers to David as "ungodly" while he was in mortal sin (4:5), but

---

152. Acts 13:22; 1 Sam 13:14. For Protestants to argue that David wasn't really saved at this moment accuses Scripture of the grossest deceptions (e.g., saying David had God's Spirit when he really did not) and God of play-acting (e.g., saying David was a man after God's heart when he really was not).
153. Cf. 1 Sam 16:13; 17:37; 18:28; 23:10–12; 30:8; 2 Sam 2:1–2; 6:9–15; 7:18–29.

then describes David's repentance as a moment in which God "reckoned [credited] righteousness" to him (vv. 6–7). In other words, God evaluated David's righteousness by examining his soul, and David recognized the same when he cried in repentance, "Create in me a clean heart, O God, and put a new and right spirit within me."[154]

Given David's relationship with God prior to his committing mortal sins, we can conclude that his confession of these sins was not the first time God "credited him with righteousness." In fact, David had confessed other sins to God prior to his sins against Bathseba and Uriah, which we see in Psalm 25: "Remember not the sins of my youth, or my transgressions; Consider my affliction and my trouble, and forgive all my sins" (vv. 7,18). This tells us that David must have also been "credited with righteousness" at these moments as well, prior to falling into mortal sin and being "credited" with righteousness again in Romans 4:5.[155]

Paul's analysis in Romans 4 teaches us that David's salvation was a process that involved being in a state of righteousness, followed by being in a state of mortal sin, followed by repenting and being restored to righteousness once again. God continued to work with David by giving him grace and perfecting his righteousness through repentance. As we

---

154. Ps. 51:10. Because David's fall from justification is so problematic for Protestants, some argue that Paul is not referring to David in Romans 4:7, but rather to a plurality of unidentified but regenerated sinners, because the referenced Psalm (31:1) says "Blessed are they (in the plural) whose iniquities are forgiven." This is a silly argument, for Paul in Romans 4:6 refers to the "man (singular/David) to whom God reputeth justice," and Romans 4:8 (Psalm 31:2) also says "Blessed is the man (singular/David) to whom the Lord hath not imputed sin."

155. We can also refer to the Apostle Peter, who was blessed by Christ (Mt 16:18), fell from grace (Mt 26:75; Mk 14:72; Jn 18:17, 25–27) and then restored to grace by Christ through confession and repentance (Jn 21:15–17).

recall from the Apostle John, if we confess our sins, then our faithful Lord will forgive them and cleanse us from all unrighteousness. (Cf. 1 Jn 1:9). This means that each time we repent of our sins, God restores us to grace and "credits" us with righteousness (that is, He sees the righteousness within us by His grace).

Paul's evaluation of David in Romans 4 also gives us two other important facts. First, righteous people in the state of grace can fall from salvation, through sin. This happened even to David, a man with the Spirit of God and an instrument of His divine revelation. Second, faith alone is insufficient for salvation, because after David committed mortal sin, he still had faith in God, but had to be restored by repenting and making satisfaction for his sins. If David did not repent, he would have been condemned, notwithstanding his faith in God. Both these truths are in clear contradiction to mainline Protestant theology.

More on the Salvation Process

Paul describes salvation as a process elsewhere in Scripture. For example, Paul writes, "Though our outer nature is wasting away, our inner nature is being renewed every day." (2 Cor 4:16). Our "inner nature" refers to our soul, which is "renewed" by grace as we persevere in lives of charity. Paul also says that we "are being changed into his likeness from one degree of glory to another; for this comes from the Lord who is the Spirit." (2 Cor 3:18). Being "changed into His likeness" refers to the inner man, and the merits we receive in this life are translated into the glory of the next.

Because salvation is a process, Paul says we are "being

saved" (present tense) over the course of our lives.[156] This refers to our earthly journey as we persevere in God's grace. Paul also says that "we will be saved" (future tense).[157] This refers to our heavenly journey when we pass from this life to the next. When John says that "no murderer has eternal life abiding in him," this "eternal life" refers to the sanctifying grace in the soul, not the vision of God in heaven. (1 Jn 3:15). "Eternal life" commences with the infusion of grace at baptism, and is actualized in eternity with the Beatific Vision.

If Christ died once, how is salvation a process? It is a process because Christ's atoning work is a process. Scripture makes this truth very clear. Even though Jesus died "once for all," He also appears "once for all" in heaven to intercede for us—for the purpose of saving us.[158] Paul says, "Consequently he is able for all time to save those who draw near to God through him, since he always lives to make intercession for them." (Heb 7:25). Paul also connects justification with Christ's ongoing mediation before the Father when he writes: "It is God who justifies; who is to condemn? Is it Christ Jesus, who died, yes, who was raised from the dead, who is at the right hand of God, who indeed intercedes for us?" (Rom 8:33–34).

If Christ's work is "finished," as most Protestants contend, then why does Jesus continue to intercede for us to save us? Aren't we already saved by "faith alone"? Doesn't any kind of intercession take away from "the finished work of the cross"? If we really have been imputed Christ's righteousness by a one-time profession of faith in His work, then Jesus' heavenly intercession is superfluous. If "faith alone"

---

156. Col 1:18; 2 Cor 2:15.
157. Mt 10:22; 24:13; Mk 13:13; 16:16; Acts 15:11; Rom 5:9–10; 1 Cor 3:15; 5:5; Jas 5:15.
158. Cf. Heb 7:27; 10:10; Heb 9:12.

were sufficient to apply the merits of Christ's atoning death to the sinner, then these verses wouldn't make any sense. No, these verses about Christ's ongoing intercession make sense only when we understand that salvation is a process.

Christ continually intercedes for us because we continually need God's grace for salvation. Christ secures this grace for us by appearing before his Father as "a Lamb standing, as though it had been slain." (Rev 5:6). Although He died once, Jesus our High Priest enters heaven with "something to offer" by "taking his own blood" into the "Holy Place."[159] Hence, Jesus makes His "sacrifice for sin" eternally present before the throne of His Father, and the Father responds by granting grace to His children who need it. After Paul describes Jesus' heavenly priesthood, he says, "Let us then with confidence draw near to the throne of grace, that we may receive mercy and find grace to help in time of need." (Heb 4:16).

When is this time of need? It is for our entire lives. Why? Because salvation is a process. We need God's grace to master concupiscence, to renounce our sin, and to pay the debts of temporal punishment we owe to God. We need grace to confess our sins so that there "remains a sacrifice for sin" to be forgiven of them. (Heb 10:26). We need grace to "share in his holiness," which is necessary for eternal life. We need grace to persevere in faith, hope, and charity to the end of our lives. We need grace to live like Abraham lived. In short, we need grace to be perfect, as our heavenly Father is perfect.

For most of us, spiritual perfection is rarely reached this side of heaven. Habitual venial sin, unconquered sinful inclinations, and debts of satisfaction for sin stain the soul and bar our entry into heaven where nothing defiled can exist.

---

159. Heb 8:3; 9:12. For an in-depth look at Christ's priestly mediation in heaven, see my book *The Biblical Basis for the Eucharist* (Our Sunday Visitor).

Nevertheless, if we die in God's grace but fail to attain perfection in this life, God in His mercy has provided purgatory as the means of attaining the necessary perfection in the next. We will analyze the biblical basis for the doctrine of Purgatory in more detail in the next chapter.

PROOF FROM SCRIPTURE
AND THE FATHERS

W E NOW look at the scriptural verses that teach specifically about purgatory. Like most of the core doctrines of the Christian faith, many (but not all) of the verses about purgatory allude to the doctrine implicitly, but not explicitly. This should not cast doubt upon the divine and apostolic origin of the doctrine. Most of the dogmas of Christianity are found only implicitly in Scripture. This is because God has revealed His Word in both Scripture and Tradition and not Scripture alone.

We see this with the most fundamental dogma of the Christian faith—the dogma of the Blessed Trinity. No Protestant is able to point to the verse or verses that teach that there are three divine persons in the one God, each of whom is also God. The Christological doctrines, specifically concerning the two natures and two wills of Christ, are also not explicit in Scripture. No verse tells us that Christ has two distinct natures or two distinct wills. It took the Catholic Church centuries to define these dogmas as she evaluated both Scripture and Tradition, just as it took her centuries to define the canon of Scripture.[160]

---

160. The Catholic Church defined the dogmas of the Blessed Trinity at the

This means that the Scriptures may be considered materially sufficient, but not formally sufficient, to teach the doctrines of the faith. "Material sufficiency" means that Scripture contains all the "materials" necessary to give us true doctrine. In other words, Scripture contains all the required "bricks" for building the dogmatic structure. However, sources outside of Scripture (namely, the oral apostolic Tradition and the Church) are often necessary to give form to the true meaning of the dogma. The Tradition, you might say, is the mortar that connects the bricks of Scripture, and the Church is the master builder who puts it all together.[161]

This concept of the material sufficiency of Scripture is to be distinguished from the Protestant's view of Scripture's formal sufficiency. Formal sufficiency means that all the materials in Scripture are in "user-ready" form; that the structure—the bricks and mortar—have already been put together. In other words, that the doctrines in Scripture are presented in such a clear and understandable way that neither Tradition nor the Church is necessary to understand their true meaning. Of course, both history and the existence of 30,000 different Protestants denominations tend to undercut such a theory! Moreover, Protestants themselves are inconsistent in the way they apply their belief in formal sufficiency. For as we will see below, there is more explicit scriptural evidence for the dogma of purgatory (which most Protestants do not accept) than there is for the dogmas of the Trinity and Christology (which all Protestants do accept).

Council of Nicea (A.D. 325), the two natures of Christ at the Council of Chalcedon (A.D. 451), and the divine and human wills of Christ at the Third Council of Constantinople (A.D. 680–681).

161. For a detailed examination of the authority of Scripture and Tradition, see my book *The Biblical Basis for Tradition* (Our Sunday Visitor).

Interpreting the Scriptures

The Church's principal method of scriptural interpretation is based on the literal sense of the text.[162] This is because God means what He says and is not trying to deceive us. Hence, the Church teaches that we are not to depart from the literal meaning of the text unless the interpretation is untenable, or necessity requires it. This is why many passages of Scripture explicitly reveal fundamental Catholic doctrines when interpreted in their literal and obvious sense. (E.g., Matthew 16:18–19; 19:9; 26:26–28; John 3:5; 6:51–58; 20:23; 1Pet 3:21; James 2:24; 5:14–15). This approach to God's Word, which is the most reasonable one of all, resounds in the souls of those Protestants who eventually become Catholic. The literal method is also the way in which the early Church Fathers interpreted Scripture. In fact, the Church teaches that we are not to depart from the interpretation of the Fathers on a matter of the faith when they are unanimous (and they were unanimous in their belief in purgatory).[163]

In addition to the literal sense, the Church also employs the spiritual sense in its exegesis of Scripture. The spiritual sense is composed of the allegorical, the moral, and the anagogical senses.[164] The allegorical refers to the spiritual and symbolic significance of the text (often through the use of types and metaphors); the moral refers to the ways in which the text leads us to act justly; and, the anagogical sense refers to the text's eternal significance. Many of the verses alluding to purgatory are interpreted in the spiritual sense: for

---

162. This is the rule of St. Augustine, adopted by the Church (see, for example, Pope Leo XIII's *Providentissimus Deus*; CCC 116).

163. Council of Trent, *Decree Concerning the Canonical Scriptures*, Session 4 (April 8, 1546); First Vatican Council, Session 3, Chapter 2, *On Revelation* (April 24, 1870), No. 5.

164. CCC, 116–117.

example, fear of the prison (allegorical) of purgatory helps us to live holy lives (moral) as we approach the Day of Judgment (anagogical). We will keep these senses in mind as we proceed with our analysis.

Let us first examine the relevant scriptures and then look at the apostolic Tradition which has been preserved in the writings of the early Church Fathers.

The Teachings of Jesus

Matthew 5:25–26: The Judge Will Put Us in Prison

We have already referred to this teaching of Jesus a number of times. After Jesus preaches the Beatitudes, and about how our own righteousness (not His imputed righteousness) must exceed that of the Pharisees,[165] He issues warnings about who "shall be liable to judgment." (Mt 5:22). Then Jesus says,

> Make friends quickly with your accuser, while you are going with him to court, lest your accuser hand you over to the judge, and the judge to the guard, and you be put in prison; truly I say to you, you will never get out till you have paid the last penny.[166]

The first thing we note is that Jesus in this passage is teaching by using metaphors. A metaphor is something that represents or denotes something else in reality. It is figurative language that has an underlying meaning. Hence, to properly exegete the passage, we must identify what the

---

165. Cf. Mt 5:20.
166. Mt 5:25–26; see also Mt 18:30–34; Lk 12:58–59. Note that Jesus completes His teachings in Matthew chapter 5 by declaring: "You, therefore, must be perfect, as your heavenly Father is perfect" (v. 48).

metaphors in the passage represent. This is done by examining how Scripture elsewhere uses the same language.

We first note that Jesus is teaching about judgment and its
consequent penalty, prison. Every other time Jesus teaches
about "judgment" in the New Testament, He is teaching
about God's judgment upon sinners, and usually in the context of either the Particular or General Judgment.[167] In fact,
this is the fundamental principle underlying Jesus' entire
Sermon on the Mount. There is nothing in the text to sug-
gest that Jesus is speaking about temporal matters in verses
25–26 and spiritual matters in the rest of His discourse.
Hence, we can assume that Matthew 5:25–26 is about the
judgment of the person's soul at death.

Jesus begins by saying, "Make friends quickly with your
accuser." The word "accuser" (Greek, *antídikos*) is used only
three other times in the New Testament: once in Luke 12:58
(which is the related passage to Matthew 5:25–26), once in
Luke 18:3 (which refers to a parable about a civil "adversary"
in court), and once in 1 Peter 5:8 (which refers to "the devil"
and how he seeks to ruin souls). The passage from Peter,
then, is most relevant because it is explicitly connected
with the spiritual and the soul. The passage is also relevant
because it provides the only New Testament definition of
"accuser": the devil. Peter says, "Your adversary (*antídikos*)
the devil prowls around like a roaring lion, seeking someone
to devour."

Scripture teaches that Satan prowls around in an effort to
accuse mankind of sin before God and steal souls for hell.
Zechariah reveals a vision of "Joshua the high priest standing

---

167. Cf. Mt 5:21–22; 7:2; 10:15; 11:22, 24; 12:36, 41–42; Lk 10:14; 11:31–32;
　　Jn 3:19; 5:22, 24, 27, 29, 30; 9:39; 12:31; 16:8, 11. The only exception is in
　　Jn 7:24, but Jesus in this verse is not talking about judgment in the context
　　of sin and punishment.

before the angel of the Lord, and Satan standing at his right hand to accuse him." (3:1). We also read how Satan attempted to "accuse" Job of sin. (Job 1:6–12). The Book of Revelation also reveals, "Now the salvation and the power and the kingdom of our God and the authority of his Christ have come, for the accuser of our brethren has been thrown down, who accuses them day and night before our God."[168] In this verse, the accuser is Satan who has been "thrown down" to the earth to "make war" on Christians to seize their souls.[169]

In Matthew 5:25–26, Jesus is referring to Satan when He says "accuser." When He tells us to make friends with the "accuser" before going to court, Jesus is not telling us to befriend Satan, but to settle our score with him by renouncing all of his empty promises in this life so that we do not have to be accused by him before the Judge in the next life. Many saints have said that both one's guardian angel and Satan are present at the Particular Judgment, with our angel revealing to Christ our good deeds and Satan accusing us of our bad deeds. This is how the "accuser" will hand us over to the "Judge." Jesus Christ is the "lawgiver and judge" to whom all judgment has been given by the Father.[170] The ability to "make friends" with Satan also means that we can grow in virtue and holiness and make satisfaction for our sins by overcoming his temptations. In other words, we can use Satan to our advantage in this life.

Jesus' use of the phrase "going with" the devil to court affirms the same thought. Our journey to the "court" of God, the Particular Judgment, will involve battling Satan during our life. We do not want to wait until we get to court

---

168. Rev 12:10. In this verse, the Greek transliteration for "accuser" is *kategoreo* which is a synonym for *antidíkos*.
169. Cf. Rev 12:9, 12–13, 17.
170. Cf. Jas 4:12; 5:9; Jn 5:22; 2 Tim 4:1.

(the Particular Judgment) to renounce him, because then, the Judge will be in charge of the proceedings. As we have learned, the time for contrition and mercy is in this life. Once we pass to the next life, we face only God's strict and exacting justice. If we have not dealt sufficiently with the devil in this life (renouncing sin and making due satisfaction to God), we will have to do so in the "prison" of the next life. Jesus urges us to make friends quickly, because the debt owed to God is easier to pay in this life than in the next, and "time is short!" (Rev 12:12).

Because the "accuser" and "judge" are in the spiritual world, the "prison" Jesus refers to is also in the spiritual world. The New Testament uses the word "prison" in a spiritual context only two other times: in Peter's first Epistle and the Book of Revelation. Peter recalls how Christ "went and preached to the spirits in prison" after His death and before His resurrection.[171] This "prison" refers to a temporary state after death, which was not either heaven or hell. Similarly, in Revelation Jesus tells the Christians at Smyrna, "Do not fear what you are about to suffer. Behold, the devil is about to throw some of you into prison, that you may be tested, and for ten days you will have tribulation. Be faithful unto death, and I will give you the crown of life."[172]

In this verse, Jesus associates "prison" with a temporary abode of "suffering" where the righteous are "tested" for a time. In Matthew's related passage (18:34), regarding the parable of the wicked servant, Jesus says that servant is delivered "to the torturers until he paid all the debt."[173] Thus, the

---

171. I Pet 3:19. See also I Pet 4:6. Just as Peter refers to the "spirits in prison," Paul refers to the "spirits of just men made perfect" (Heb 12:23), which, as we will see below, is also an allusion to purgatory.

172. 2:10. The Greek transliteration for "prison" (*phulake*) is the same word used in Mt 5:25; I Pet 3:19; Rev 2:10; 20:7.

173. Mt 18:34 (DR).

spiritual (not literal) use of "prison" in the New Testament always refers to a place of temporal punishment for departed souls. In light of these precedents, then, we can conclude that the "prison" of Matthew 5:25–26 is also a place of temporal punishment for departed souls—or, purgatory.

The case would be even stronger if we could demonstrate that the debt the accused pays to get out of the prison refers to his sins. And we can. We have already shown that the devil seeks to accuse the prisoner of sin, and it is this debt of sin that keeps the prisoner detained. But Scripture also expressly equates "debt" (Greek, *opheilonti*) with "sin" (Greek, *hamartias*). For example, Luke's version of the Our Father says, "and forgive us our sins; for we ourselves forgive every one who is indebted to us." (11:4). Matthew also records, "And forgive us our debts, As we also have forgiven our debtors." (6:12). This demonstrates that Matthew and Luke are referring to paying the "debt of sin." This also means that the payment in Matthew 5:25–26 is to make satisfaction for sin—the very purpose of purgatory.

We further note that Jesus requires the sinner to pay the last "penny" before he can be released from the prison. A "penny" (Greek, *kodranten*) was one of the smallest denominations of money that existed during Jesus' time. This denomination was equivalent to one sixty-fourth of a denarius (a day's wage). This is also significant. It demonstrates that even the slightest faults will have to be expiated in the prison of purgatory. God's holiness and justice and the purity of His heaven demand no less. In the same gospel, Jesus says, "I tell you, on the day of judgment men will render account for every careless word they utter." (Mt 12:36).

To deny the passage's obvious connection to purgatory, Protestants often argue that the prison of Matthew 5:25 is really the hell of the damned (in so doing, they admit that the passage has underlying spiritual meanings that must be interpreted). They argue that the Greek phrase for "till" (*heos an*) continues the action of the main verb "you will never get out." If "till" does continue the action of the main verb, then the "you will never get out" action is ongoing, which means that the person is in hell, for he will "never get out" of hell. How do Catholics respond to this technical argument?

The Greek use of *heos* (until) does not mandate this conclusion. In some cases, *heos* continues the action of the main verb, and in other cases, it terminates the action. Matthew provides both usages in his Gospel, which means that the Protestant cannot prove his case on mere textual grounds.[174] In fact, over seventy-five percent of the time *heos* is used in the New Testament, it terminates the action of the main verb. The percentage is even higher when examining the Septuagint (Greek) translation of the Old Testament. If *heos* in Matthew 5:26 terminates the action of the verb "will never get out," then that means the person will get out of the prison, after he has paid his debt.

How can we definitively resolve the meaning of *heos* in Matthew 5:26? We do so by examining the context of the passage. We first note that, outside of Matthew 5:25–26 and its related passages, the word "prison" is used sixty-one times in the New Testament, yet it never refers to the hell of the reprobate. The Protestant, therefore, is attempting to define "prison" in a way that Scripture never does. Even colloquially, the term "prison" refers to a place where someone must serve a sentence and, after he does, he is set free. Nothing in Matthew 5 indicates that Jesus is using the word "prison" in a manner other than its plain meaning.

---

174. See, for example, Mt 13:33; 17:9; 18:30 where heos terminates the action of the main verb, and Mt 1:25; 11:12; 14:22; 18:34; 26:36; 28:20 where it continues the action.

Jesus' metaphorical use of money and debt (paying the last penny) also demonstrates that the man's stay in "prison" is temporary. On the money side, because people have only a finite amount of funds, and the purpose of the person's incarceration is to pay funds to satisfy debt, it follows that his stay in prison is terminated when he runs out of funds (that is, when he is finished making satisfaction). Jesus' use of the last penny also indicates that, at some point, there will be nothing left to pay and thus no further detainment will be required. On the debt side, because debt in Scripture is a metaphor for sin and indebtedness is a finite condition, means that the sin (represented by the debt) is also finite. In other words, the sin being satisfied is venial and thus the punishment is temporal. This satisfaction is unnecessary in heaven and impossible in hell, which means the prisoner is in purgatory.

Finally, we note that scriptural references to the punishments of hell are never described in the context of money or paying debt. Paying debt is a temporal punishment only. This further underscores that Matthew 5:25–26 is about making satisfaction for temporal punishments (for venial and forgiven mortal sin) which restores us to the equality of God's justice and friendship. As we will see below, Tertullian, Cyprian of Carthage, Lactantius, Basil, Ambrose, Augustine and Caesar of Arles also interpreted Matthew 5:25–26 to be a metaphorical description of purgatory. For these reasons, the great weight of the exegetical evidence supports the Catholic interpretation.

Matthew 12:32:
Forgiveness in This Age or the Next

In the verses that both precede and follow Matthew 12:32, Jesus is speaking about soteriological issues: God, Satan, merits, and judgment.[175] Sandwiched in between Jesus' teaching is His warning about blasphemy against the Holy Spirit. Jesus says,

> Therefore I tell you, every sin and blasphemy will be forgiven men, but the blasphemy against the Spirit will not be forgiven. And whoever says a word against the Son of man will be forgiven; but whoever speaks against the Holy Spirit will not be forgiven, either in this age or in the age to come.[176]

The plain meaning of Jesus' words is obvious. Jesus declares that there is forgiveness both "in this age and in the age to come." If the phrase "age to come" refers to life after death, then this passage must refer to purgatory. That is because forgiveness is unnecessary in heaven and impossible in hell. To properly exegete this passage, then, we have to understand what the phrase "in the age to come" means.

The identical Greek phrase ("in this age or the age to come") is used only one other time in the New Testament, in Ephesians 1:21, where Paul describes Jesus' name as "above every name that is named, not only in this age but also in that which is to come."[177] Let us look at the context of this verse from Ephesians. In the previous verse 20, Paul describes the risen Christ as sitting at the Father's "right hand in the

---

175. Mt 12:26–29; 33–37.
176. Mt 12:31–32.
177. The Greek transliteration of the phrase in both Mt 12:32 and Eph 1:21 is: *"en touto to aioni oute ento mellonti."*

heavenly places," and, in verse 22, how the Father "has put all things under his feet and has made him the head over all things for the church, which is his body, the fullness of him who fills all in all."

This means that the "age to come" in Ephesians 1:21 refers to the afterlife where Jesus intercedes in heaven as High Priest before the Father.[178] This also means that there is forgiveness in the afterlife. In fact, every time the New Testament uses the phrase "age to come," it refers to the afterlife.[179]

Ephesians 1:21 provides us other insights about Matthew 12:32's connection to purgatory. First, the verse in Ephesians (1:21) says Jesus' name "is *above every name.*" This is the same phrase that Paul uses in Philippians 2:10 when he says that God "bestowed on him the name which is above every name." This is significant because Paul is describing the importance of Jesus' name in "the age to come" in Ephesians 1:21, and its importance to those "under the earth" in Philippians 2:10.

As we have seen, the abode "under the earth" may be seen as a reference to the "Church Suffering" in purgatory. This connects those "in the age to come" with those "under the earth"—that is, those in the afterlife who are subject to Christ's heavenly reign.[180] Those "in the age to come" are said to be "under his feet" (Eph 1:22) and those "under the earth" are said to "bend the knee" (Phil 2:10) at the name of Jesus. This means that those in Matthew 12:32 who are forgiven in "the age to come" are the same people who are "under the earth"—two allusions to the abode of purgatory.

Second, Ephesians 1:22 makes reference to "the church, which is his body," which, given the context, is also a reference

---

178. See also Rom 8:34; Acts 7:55–56; Col 3:1; Heb 8:1; 10:12; 12:2; 1 Pet 3:22.
179. E.g., Mk 10:30, Lk 18:30, Lk 20:35–36, Heb 6:5.
180. Cf. Eph 1:20–22; Phil 2:9.

to the Church in the afterlife (because it exists in "the age to come" where God "has put all things under His feet"). We have seen Paul make the same reference to Christ's "body, the church" in Colossians 1:24 when he says, "I rejoice in my sufferings for your sake, and in my flesh I complete what is lacking in Christ's afflictions for the sake of his body, that is, the church."

Because Paul is speaking of the same Church (for there is only one Church) in both Ephesians 1:22 and Colossians 1:24, means that Paul can suffer for the sake of the Church in "the age to come," the same "Church Suffering" that is "under the earth." That is, Paul can suffer for the souls in purgatory. As we will continue to see, our sufferings atone not only for sin and temporal punishments in this life, but also give rise to "forgiveness in the age to come." (Mt 12:32). Hence, there is a clear, scriptural connection between "suffering," "church," "body," "under the earth," and "age to come"—all references to purgatory. Augustine, Jerome, Pope Gregory, and Pope Gelasius also interpreted Matthew 12:32 as a reference to purgatory.

The possibility of forgiveness in the age to come supports the Catholic and Scriptural teaching about venial sin. As John teaches, there is sin "which is mortal" and sin "which is not mortal." (1 Jn 5:16–17). Because mortal sin kills the life of grace in the soul, it cannot be forgiven in "the age to come" when the soul's time for contrition has passed. Mortal sin must be confessed and absolved in this life. Because venial sin is harmful but not deadly, it is forgiven in the "age to come," according to the plain words of our Savior.

But if they want to maintain their objection to purgatory, Protestants must deny these plain words of Jesus. To that end, Protestants will often argue that in Matthew 12:32 Jesus was simply trying to emphasize the gravity of the sin of blasphemy against the Holy Spirit. In other words, Jesus didn't really mean there was forgiveness in "the age to come," only that blasphemy against the Holy Ghost would *never* be forgiven. They point to a related passage in Mark 3:29 where Jesus says, "but whoever blasphemes against the Holy Spirit never has forgiveness, but is guilty of an eternal sin."

The Protestant argument, of course, denies the plain and literal meaning of Jesus' words. It would be superfluous for Jesus to say there is no forgiveness for blasphemy against the Holy Spirit in "the age to come" if there wasn't a possibility of *any* forgiveness in "the age to come." Moreover, because there really *is* an "age to come," this would make Jesus' statement misleading if not deceptive. Jesus didn't need to fabricate a phony stage of forgiveness to emphasize the gravity of the sin against the Spirit, and no one in the early Church ever believed otherwise.

It should also be noted that the Protestant argument misunderstands the meaning of the "unforgivable sin." While it is true that blasphemy against the Holy Spirit is an "eternal sin," all mortal sins are eternal sins because they merit eternal damnation unless God forgives them before death. The sacrifice of Jesus Christ is sufficient to atone for all sins—even blasphemies against the Holy Spirit—so long as the sinner repents in this life. Hence, the Church has always understood Jesus' warning to apply only to those people who die unrepentant. That is, blasphemy against the Holy Spirit means rejecting God's mercy and forgiveness, which is called impenitence.[181] God does not forgive this sin because the sinner does not want forgiveness. In this sense, then, the sin is "unforgivable."

---

181. Augustine held that the unforgivable sin was final impenitence. Athanasius, Hilary, Ambrose, Jerome, and Chrysostom held that the unforgivable sin was literally to utter a blasphemy against the Holy Spirit.

Luke 12:47–48:
Some Servants Receive Only a Light Beating

In Luke's Gospel, chapter 12, Jesus teaches a parable about the master and his servants—another spiritual teaching about the consequences of sin. In the parable, Jesus warns His servants to be ready for His coming, "for the Son of man is coming at an hour you do not expect" (v. 40). In describing the potential punishments that unprepared servants could suffer at the Master's coming, Jesus says

> But if that servant says to himself, "My master is delayed in coming," and begins to beat the menservants and the maidservants, and to eat and drink and get drunk, the master of that servant will come on a day when he does not expect him and at an hour he does not know, and will punish him and put him with the unfaithful. And that servant who knew his master's will, but did not make ready or act according to his will, shall receive a severe beating. But he who did not know, and did what deserved a beating, shall receive a light beating.

Generally, when Jesus talks about punishing sinners at His "coming," He is talking about His Second Coming at the General Judgment, and not the sinner's Particular Judgment (although a person's Particular Judgment is a form of "coming" as well). However, because the passage refers to the Master's coming on "the day," the passage could be about the servants' Particular Judgment.[182] Whether this parable is about the General Judgment or the Particular Judgment, it is a strong allusion to purgatory. Why? It is because Jesus is

---

182. Cf. 1 Cor 1:18; 3:14; 5:5; 2 Tim 4:8; Heb 10:25 where "day" refers to one's Particular Judgment.

referring to temporal punishments for the saved in the next life, or in "the age to come."

Jesus first mentions the wicked servant who committed mortal sins of commission, namely, assaulting his servants and getting drunk. Scripture teaches that such sins deserve eternal condemnation.[183] In regard to this servant, Jesus says He "will punish him and put him with the unfaithful" (v. 46). Jesus uses this word for "punish" (Greek, *dichotomeo*) only one other time in the New Testament, in the related passage Matthew 24:51, which regards the same wicked servant who beat his servants and got drunk: "the master of that house will come . . . and will punish him, and put him with the hypocrites; there men will weep and gnash their teeth."[184] The "hypocrites" (Greek, *apistos*) are the unbelievers whose "lot shall be in the lake that burns with fire and brimstone." (Rev 21:8). This means that Jesus in Luke 12 is talking about punishment in the afterlife.

However, Jesus also mentions the two servants who committed venial sins of omission. The first servant knew his Master's will but failed to act according to it, and Jesus says this servant "shall receive a severe beating." The second servant also failed to do His Master's will, but was ignorant of His will because he "did not know" it. Jesus says this servant "shall receive a light beating." Jesus in His parables uses this word for "beating" (*dero*) six other times, and it always refers to temporal, not eternal, punishment.[185] In fact, the other instances in the New Testament where *dero* is used refer exclusively to temporal punishments or penance.[186]

---

183. 1 Cor 5:11; 6:10; Gal 5:21; Eph 5:18.
184. The Greek *dichotomeo* literally means "to cut in half." See also Mt 8:12; 13:42, 50; 22:13; 25:30; Lk 13:28 where "putting away" sinners at the General Judgment refers to eternal damnation.
185. Mt 21:35; Mk 12:3, 5; 13:9; Lk 20:10–11.
186. Cf. Lk 22:63; Jn 18:23; Acts 5:40; 16:37; 22:19; 1 Cor 9:26; 2 Cor 11:20.

Thus, Jesus makes a clear distinction between temporal and eternal punishments in the life to come. Those who sin mortally will receive the eternal punishment of damnation. Those who sin only venially will receive temporal punishments to make satisfaction for their sins, but will still be saved—they will not be "put with the unfaithful." Further, those who commit venial sins will be punished in proportion to their offense. Those who were ignorant of God's will are less culpable that those who were not, and thus, the ignorant servants will receive a "light beating," while the lazy servants will receive a "severe beating." In short, Jesus presents a continuum of punishment in the afterlife—either eternal or temporal—depending upon the person's deeds.

Because Jesus' parable is in the context of His Second Coming also demonstrates that there is pain and suffering in the afterlife for those who are destined for heaven. As John reveals in the Book of Revelation, "he will wipe away every tear from their eyes, and death shall be no more, neither shall there be mourning nor crying nor pain any more, for the former things have passed away." (21:4). This elimination of pain and suffering—which according to Revelation is happening in eternity—occurs only after Christ creates a "new heaven and a new earth," when "the first earth had passed away, and the sea was no more" (v. 1).

It is interesting to note that Luke 12:47–48 references Deuteronomy 25:1–3. This related Old Testament passage says,

> If there is a dispute between men, and they come into court, and the judges decide between them, acquitting the innocent and condemning the guilty, then if the guilty man deserves to be beaten, the judge shall cause him to lie down and be beaten

in his presence with a number of stripes in proportion to his offense. Forty stripes may be given him, but not more; lest, if one should go on to beat him with more stripes than these, your brother be degraded in your sight.

It seems certain that Jesus was drawing from Deuteronomy 25 in both His teachings in Matthew 5:25–26 and Luke 12:47–48. In describing the punishment of the sinner, Jesus uses "judge" and "court" (Matthew 5) and "beating" (Luke 12). Jesus also alludes to the punishment being "in proportion to his offense" ("severe" versus "light" beatings in Luke 12). Jesus' clear connection to Deuteronomy 25 is important because it further underscores that He is describing temporal punishments in Matthew 5 and Luke 12 (just as they are temporal in Deuteronomy 25). Moreover, both the punishments in Matthew 5 and Luke 12 are imposed in the afterlife (in Matthew 5, at the "judgment"; in Luke 12, at the Master's "coming"). These connections further support the Catholic doctrine of purgatory.

The Good Thief's Salvation
Does Not Disprove Purgatory

When examining Jesus' teachings in the context of purgatory, Protestants often bring up how Jesus forgave the Good Thief during the crucifixion. They believe that Jesus' spontaneous gift of salvation for the thief denies any need for purgatory. We recall that when the thief asked Jesus to remember him when Jesus came into His kingdom, Jesus responded to him by saying, "Truly, I say to you, today you will be with me in Paradise." (Lk 23:43). Protestants use this extraordinary event to deny not only the doctrine of purgatory, but also the

Catholic doctrines concerning the necessity of baptism and good works for salvation. Yet Jesus' isolated statement during this unusual event does nothing of the sort.

On the most basic level, Jesus' statement doesn't necessarily preclude the Good Thief from having to go to purgatory before joining Jesus in "Paradise." The thief, upon his death, may certainly have had to go through additional purification before entering heaven on that same day.[187] We must also remember that purgatory is for those souls who still owe God satisfaction for their sins. But the Good Thief does a number of things suggesting that he would have already made sufficient satisfaction for his sin before his death.

For example, the Good Thief recognizes that he and the other criminal "are receiving the due reward of our deeds." (Lk 23:42). In other words, Scripture reveals that the Good Thief's punishment of crucifixion was the due debt he owed to God for his crimes. In prior verses the Good Thief also rebuked the other thief who was reviling Jesus and expressed his "fear" of God. He also recognized that Jesus "has done nothing wrong." After the thief confesses both His guilt and Jesus' goodness, he asks Jesus for salvation: "Jesus, remember me when you come in your kingly power."

Thus, the Good Thief repents of his sins and exhibits faith, hope, and charity to the moment of his death. When we couple these factors with his painful demise, we may conclude that the Good Thief was completely purified of his sins, and this is why Jesus blessed him with salvation. That would mean that the Good Thief would have had no need for purgatory, for his debt of punishment was satisfied on his cross. The thief's actions also prevent one's asserting that

---

187. The Good Thief would have actually gone to Abraham's bosom until Christ opened the gates of heaven with His Ascension. Thus, Jesus uses the word "Paradise" in Luke 23:43 in this broader sense.

he was saved by "faith alone," for his faith, like that of David, was accompanied by sorrow for his sin, hope in God, and charity toward his fellow man.[188]

The Teachings of Paul

In addition to the Lord Jesus, the Apostle Paul also provides us with a number of teachings that support the doctrine of purgatory. In fact, his teaching in 1 Corinthians 3 is perhaps the most explicit teaching on purgatory in all of the New Testament. Most of the early Church Fathers (such as Clement of Alexandria, Origen, Gregory of Nyssa, Augustine, and Pope Gregory the Great) interpreted Paul's teaching to be a clear reference to purgatory. We begin by looking at this most critical passage.

1 Corinthians 3:10–17:
We May Be Saved Only as through Fire

Before we examine the passage, we first look at some background. At the very beginning of his letter, Paul makes it clear that the Corinthians are "saved" Christians. In the first chapter Paul says he is writing "to those sanctified in Christ Jesus" who have been given "the grace of God" and who "are not lacking in any spiritual gift." Because their sanctification is a process as they respond to God's grace, Paul affirms that the Corinthians "are being saved." (1 Cor 1:2–18).

Notwithstanding their exalted position, Paul points

---

188. The Good Thief did not require baptism because (1) he was unable to be baptized and God doesn't punish people for failing to do the impossible; (2) he would have sought baptism if he were able and hence had a "baptism of desire"; and (3) he was still on the Old Testament side of the cross and hence the sacraments of the New Law did not yet bind the faithful.

out that worldly wisdom had trickled into the Corinthian church. In fact, in the first two chapters Paul refers to this issue of "wisdom" fifteen times.[189] The wisdom of the pagan world, which thought the Cross of Christ was folly, was corrupting Christ's gospel in Corinth.[190] This worldly wisdom was causing "dissensions" and "quarreling" among the Corinthians,[191] which Scripture elsewhere reveals are serious sins.[192] In short, even though they are currently "saved," Paul is warning the Corinthians that they are sinning against God and risking the loss of their souls.

Chapter 3 opens with Paul's repeating his warning about the Corinthians' worldliness and divisive attitudes. He says, "for you are still in the flesh. For while there is jealousy and strife among you, are you not of the flesh, and behaving like ordinary men?" (v. 3). After affirming their equality in spite of their factious ways, Paul says that "each shall receive his wages according to his labor. For we are God's fellow workers; you are God's field, God's building" (vv. 8–9). Paul then reveals the potential consequences, on the Day of Judgment, of the Corinthians' sins:

> According to the commission of God given to me, like a skilled master builder I laid a foundation, and another man is building upon it. Let each man take care how he builds upon it. For no other foundation can any one lay than that which is laid, which is Jesus Christ. Now if any one builds on the foundation with gold, silver precious stones, wood, hay, stubble—each man's work will become manifest; for the Day will disclose it, because it will

---

189. 1 Cor 1:17, 19–22, 24–27, 30; 2:1; 4–7, 13.
190. 1 Cor 1:20–2:9.
191. 1 Cor 1:10–11. See also 2 Cor 12:20.
192. Cf. Rom 1:29; 13:13; 2 Cor 12:20; Gal 5:20; 1 Tim 6:4; Jas 3:14, 16.

be revealed with fire, and the fire will test what sort of work each one has done. If the work which any man has built on the foundation survives, he will receive a reward. If any man's work is burned up, he will suffer loss, though he himself will be saved, but only as through fire. Do you not know that you are God's temple and that God's Spirit dwells in you? If any one destroys God's temple, God will destroy him. For God's temple is holy, and that temple you are.

Let us unpack this crucial passage. We first note that Paul is teaching by using a string of metaphors. As we saw in Matthew 5:25–26, this means we have to interpret the metaphors because they represent underlying truths. Paul first tells the Corinthians that they are "God's building." Then Paul says that he, as a skilled master builder, "laid a foundation" and that "each man builds upon it." Paul then says that the "foundation" is Jesus Christ. Thus, we see that Paul (a skilled master builder) laid the foundation (Jesus Christ) of the building (the Corinthians). In other words, Paul as a minister of the gospel revealed to the Corinthians the truth of Jesus Christ, who must now be the foundation of their entire lives.

Paul also says that the Corinthians, as "God's fellow workers," must build upon the foundation he laid for them. Paul explains how one can erect his building on the foundation of Christ with various types of materials—"gold," "silver," "precious stones," "wood," "hay," and "stubble." These materials are metaphors for the deeds that the Corinthians perform during their lives. The gold, silver, and precious stones represent good works, and the wood, hay, and stubble represent bad works.

Paul elsewhere connects "deeds" with "laying a foundation" to secure one's eternal "life" when he writes, "They are to do good, to be rich in good deeds, liberal and generous, thus laying up for themselves a good foundation for the future, so that they may take hold of the life which is life indeed." (2 Tim 6:19). This is why Paul says once more to the Corinthians that one "builds on the foundation," and then says, "each man's work will become manifest." The materials with which one builds on his foundation represent the person's good and bad works or deeds, and they will be subject to God's strict judgment.

In addition to calling the Corinthians "God's building," he also calls them "God's temple." Paul explains his use of this alternative metaphor when he says, "For God's temple is holy, and that temple you are." In other words, Paul is explaining to the Corinthians that they are not some ordinary building. Rather, they have become the very dwelling place of God, through the gift of grace. This is why Paul says, "Do you not know that you are God's temple and that God's Spirit dwells in you?" Later in the letter Paul also says, "Do you not know that your body is a temple of the Holy Spirit within you which you have from God?" (6:19). Because the souls of the Corinthians have literally become temples of God, Paul says, "Let each man take care how he builds upon it."

The Corinthians must be careful in building their spiritual edifice, because God will examine the structure when they die. Paul says, "for the Day will disclose it, because it will be revealed with fire, and the fire will test what sort of work each one has done." The phrase "the Day" refers to the person's Day of Judgment. Earlier in the letter, Paul says Christ will sustain the Corinthians "to the end . . . in the day of our Lord Jesus Christ," in reference to their individual judgment. (1:8). Later in the letter, Paul says he has excommunicated a member of the church so that his soul "may be saved in the day of the Lord Jesus." (5:5).

Elsewhere Paul also uses the expression when he asks God to have mercy on his friend Onesiphorus: "may the Lord grant him to find mercy from the Lord on that Day." (2 Tim 1:18). In the same letter, Paul looks to his own Particular Judgment when he says that "the Lord, the righteous judge, will award to me on that Day." (4:8). Paul further tells the Hebrews to encourage one another "all the more as you see the Day drawing near." (10:25). As Scripture also demonstrates, "the day" has a soteriological significance, referring either to the Particular or General Judgment.[193]

Thus, Paul reveals that God will judge the Corinthians according to their works on their Day of Judgment. Given his previous admonitions, it is clear that Paul has the Corinthians' sins of worldliness and factiousness on his mind. Paul affirms he is speaking of God's judgment in the next chapter when he says, "Therefore, do not pronounce judgment before the time, before the Lord comes, who will bring to light the things now hidden in darkness and will disclose the purposes of the heart. Then every man will receive his commendation from God." (1 Cor 4:5). This reiterates Paul's teaching in other passages of Scripture about God's judgment of one's works:

> For he will render to every man according to his works: to those who by patience in well-doing seek for glory and honor and immortality, he will give eternal life; but for those who are factious and

---

193. Mt 15:10; 11:22, 24; 12:36; 25:13; Lk 17:30; Rom 2:5, 16; 2 Cor 1:14; Eph 4:30; Phil 1:6, 10; 2:16; 1 Thess 5:2, 4–5, 8; 2 Thess 2:2–3; 2 Pet 3:7, 10, 12, 18; 1 Jn 4:17; Sir 18:24.

do not obey the truth, but obey wickedness, there will be wrath and fury.[194]

For we shall all stand before the judgment seat of God. . . . So each of us shall give account of himself to God. (Rom 14:10, 12).

For we must all appear before the judgment seat of Christ, so that each one may receive good or evil, according to what he has done in the body (2 Cor 5:10).

How will God judge a man's works? Paul says that God will reveal the work with fire, and "the fire will test what sort of work each one has done." (1 Cor 3:13). As we have seen, Scripture uses "fire" both metaphorically (to represent God's divine justice) and literally (to represent what God uses to purge and destroy).[195] Just as God "tests our hearts"[196] during our lives to purify and perfect us for heaven, God "tests our work" with fire after we die to evaluate how we "finished the race."[197] Thus, Paul reveals three outcomes of God's judgment after His testing by fire:

The man who built with only good materials will receive a reward.

The man who built with both good and bad materials will have his bad materials burned up by fire;

---

194. Rom 2:6–8. It is interesting to note that Paul mentions the sin of being "factious" in Rom 2:8, the very sin of which he accuses the Corinthians in 1 Cor 1:10–11; 2 Cor 12:20.

195. While Protestants generally ascribe meanings to all of the metaphors in 1 Corinthians 3, they do not ascribe a meaning to the "fire" in vv. 13, 15 because post-mortem fire in relation to the saved does not fit their theology.

196. 1 Thess 2:4; Jas 1:3. See also Heb 11:17 where Paul says Abraham was "tested" when he "offered up Isaac."

197. 2 Tim 4:7; See also 1 Cor 9:24; Heb 12:1.

he too will have to pass through the same fire but then will be saved.

The man who built with only bad materials has destroyed God's temple, and God will destroy him.

Paul says that the man who built with only good materials is saved (he receives his "reward"), and the man who built with only bad materials is condemned (he is "destroyed"). This is because the good materials represent good works and the bad materials represent evil works. This teaching reiterates the polarity of the salvation/damnation scenario that Paul describes in Romans 2:7–8 in regard to one's works: those who do good works are rewarded with "eternal life," and those who do bad works are subject to "wrath and fury." In other words, if people are condemned for bad works, then people are saved (not just rewarded) for good works.

What about the man who built with both good and bad materials? Paul explains: "If any man's work is burned up, he will suffer loss, though he himself will be saved, but only as through fire." The man "suffers loss" because some of his "work is burned up." The Greek for "suffer loss" (*zemiothesetai*) refers to punishment, which means the saved man is punished after death for his bad works. The New Testament uses this word (from the Greek verb *zemioo*) even to describe eternal punishment.[198] The Old Testament also uses the word (from the Hebrew, *anash*) to mean "penalty," "punish," or "suffer."[199] In addition, the Old Testament uses the word (*anash*/*zemioo*) to describe a monetary "fine."[200]

This means there is a connection between the "fine" of

---

198. Cf. Mt 16:26; Mk 8:36; Lk 9:25.
199. E.g., Prov 19:19, 21:11, 22:3.
200. E.g., Ex 21:22, Deut 22:19, Prov 17:26.

1 Corinthians 3:15 and the "payment of the last penny" in Matthew 5:26. Both use monetary metaphors to describe temporal punishments in the afterlife imposed for bad deeds. In the case of Matthew 5, the man is imprisoned which refers to the "pain of loss" and "pain of duration" that we previously discussed. In 1 Corinthians 3, the man suffers loss from fire which refers to the "pain of sense."

What is critical to note in 1 Corinthians 3:15 is that the man is punished after death for building with bad materials, but he is still saved. The Greek for "will be saved" (*sothese-tai*) refers to nothing less than the salvation with which God rewards the Elect at the end of their lives. Needless to say, a post-mortem punishment by fire that precedes salvation is utterly foreign to Protestant theology. If a man's sins have already been washed away by the imputed righteousness of Christ, how can he be punished for those sins after death? Because this passage is so damaging to Protestant theology, Protestant apologists have scrambled to come up with rebuttals. Let us briefly examine the most common ones.

Bad Motives, Not Sins?

Because most Protestants do not believe a saved person can be judged for his sins after death (because he was already saved by "faith alone" during his life), he is forced to ascribe another meaning to the bad materials (wood, hay, stubble) that were burned up in the fire. Thus, some Protestants argue that the bad materials are metaphors for the person's bad motives, and not his bad works. In other words, the saved Christian performed good deeds (represented by gold, silver, precious stones) during his life, but some of these deeds had less than stellar motivations (represented by wood, hay, stubble). By making this distinction between motives (for the saved) and sins/works (for the damned), the Protestant attempts to save his "faith alone" theology while denying the doctrine of purgatory.

Of course, these verses say nothing about "motivations" and thus the attempt is pure anachronism. With this argument, the Protestant creates an arbitrary dichotomy between how God judges the saved in verses 14–15 (by their motives) and how God judges the damned in verse 17 (by their sins). Moreover, from a biblical perspective, the Protestant is making a distinction without a difference. This is because Scripture teaches that bad motives are sins. In some cases, they are the worst kind of sins. As we have discussed, sin originates in the soul of man where he harbors his evil motives. These motives give rise to sin when the free will gives in to them. As James says, "then desire when it has conceived gives birth to sin; and sin when it is full-grown brings forth death." (1:15).

When Paul says in both Romans 2 and 14 that each of us will have to give an account of our deeds at the judgment seat of Christ, he repeatedly refers to the interior motive of passing "judgment" on our neighbor. In Romans 2, Paul says, "Therefore you have no excuse, O man, whoever you are, when you judge another; for in passing judgment upon him you condemn yourself" (v. 1). In Romans 14, Paul says, "Who are you to pass judgment on the servant of another? Why do you pass judgment on your brother? Or you, why do you despise your brother? Then let us no more pass judgment on one another."[201] Paul even goes on to say that "whatever does not proceed from faith is sin" (v. 23). Hence, Paul is revealing that our interior motives (here, mentally judging another) are severely judged by God, because bad motives

201. Vv. 4, 10, 13.

are sins. These are the very defects that must be rooted out in purgatory before we attain to the Beatific Vision.

We have also seen that Paul in his Letter to the Corinthians is addressing sin in the Corinthian church. In chapter 1, Paul mentions the "dissension" and "quarreling" among the Corinthians. In chapter 3, Paul says there is "jealousy and strife" among them. In his Second letter to the Corinthians, Paul classifies "quarreling" and "jealousy" as grave sins, along with the sins of anger, selfishness, slander, gossip, conceit and disorder—all, evidently, prevalent attributes of the church at Corinth. (Cf. 2 Cor 12:20).

Paul also tells the Corinthians that "there is immorality among you, and of a kind that is not found even among the pagans" (5:1) and warns that "neither the immoral, nor idolaters, nor adulterers, nor homosexuals, nor thieves, nor the greedy, nor drunkards, nor revilers, nor robbers will inherit the kingdom of God." (6:9–10). In short, Paul is telling the Corinthians that they have been committing mortal sins, not just harboring bad motivations. The Corinthians need to avoid these sins because these sins will be judged by fire and they will determine their eternal destiny. Thus, the "bad materials" metaphor in 1 Corinthians 3 refers to the Corinthians' sins, not merely their motives—both of which, by the way, are to be tested by the fire of God's divine justice.

Loss of Rewards?

Because the phrase "suffer loss" (*zemiothesetai*) in 1 Corinthians 3:15 refers to temporal punishment after death, and this post-mortem punishment for the saved is irreconcilable with Protestant theology, Protestant apologists have to neutralize the phrase. To that end, the Protestant correctly notes that the man who builds with good materials receives a reward and the man who builds with both good and bad materials suffers loss. Based on the continuum of the building metaphor, the Protestant concludes that "suffering loss" is the opposite of receiving a "reward." Thus, the Protestant is forced to equate "suffering loss" with losing "rewards," and not with temporal punishments. In other words, God is granting rewards to the man in verse 14, and removing rewards from the man in verse 15—but saving both of them. Is this what verse 15 says? No.

Verse 15 actually says, "If any man's work is burned up, he will suffer loss, though he himself will be saved, but only as through fire." It is the work that is burned up, not the reward. The person who builds with both good and bad materials does not lose his reward, because salvation is the reward.[202] Paul says that "knowing that from the Lord you will receive the inheritance as your reward; you are serving the Lord Christ."[203] Because the inheritance of heaven is the reward, the man in verse 15 did not lose it. Thus, if the man indeed receives the reward of salvation, how does he "suffer loss"? The answer to this question poses another insurmountable problem for Protestant theology.

The man "suffers loss" because he must pass through the same fire that burned up his bad works in order to be saved. As we have seen, after Paul explains that a man's work is burned up and that he will suffer loss, he goes on to say, "though he himself will be saved, but only as through fire." The Greek word for "but only" (houtos) is an adverb which

---

202. Even though salvation is the reward, the saved enjoy degrees of glory in heaven based upon the merits they gained on earth. This is why Jesus says, "yet he who is least in the kingdom of heaven is greater than he [John the Baptist]" (Mt 11:11).

203. Col 3:24. See also Heb 11:26; 2 Jn 1:8; Ps 28:4; Isa 62:11; Jer 31:16; 32:19. Based on the context, the only logical referent for the "reward" in verse 14 is the "salvation" in verse 15.

means "just as" or "in the same manner."[204] Paul uses it in the preceding chapter, in 1 Corinthians 2:11, when he says that a man doesn't comprehend the thoughts of another man, "just as" (so also) he doesn't comprehend the thoughts of God.

As applied to 1 Corinthians 3:15, the adverb "but only" (*houtos*) modifies the verb "will be saved" (*sothesetai*). The modification is directed by the adverbial clause "as through fire." This means the adverb *houtos* tells us how the man is saved: by passing through fire. Thus, the man who did bad works must, in the same manner, pass through the fire that burned up his bad works to obtain salvation. This means that the man's salvation is delayed on the basis of his works, for before being saved he must first endure a trial by fire. This is hostile to Protestant theology, which holds that works provide no basis for how one attains salvation (through fire), only how one enjoys salvation (rewards).

The man must pass through the same fire in order to be purged of the things that produced the bad works in the first place. Because the phrase "suffer loss" refers to temporal punishment, the man who passes through the fire experiences temporal punishment for the defects associated with his bad works. If there are any defects in the man's "spiritual" building (venial sin, evil inclinations, debts of punishment), the fire will consume them, just as it consumed the defective materials (wood, hay, stubble) in the physical building. As Christ Himself revealed, in the context of God's judgment of our deeds, "every one will be salted with fire." (Mk 9:49). St. Peter also warned the faithful to "think not strange the burning heat which is to try you." (1 Pet 4:12).

---

204. The New Testament uses the word *houtos* around 350 times. As an adverb, it invariably means "in the same manner," "in the same way," "in like manner," "just as," "the same," "even so," "yet so," and "also."

Thus, the scriptural and Catholic view is that works deter-mine both whether salvation is attained, and, if so, how it is attained. Works serve as a basis to advance or retard salva-tion, depending upon what materials one used to build his spiritual edifice—a concept inimical to Protestant theology.

What about the man who built with only bad materials? Paul says that he has destroyed God's temple, and thus "God will destroy him." This means that the person will be con-demned, for the fire has consumed the entire edifice and there is nothing left for God.[205] We therefore see a contin-uum in Paul's metaphor: the man who builds with only good materials is rewarded with salvation; the man who builds with both good and bad materials suffers a delay, but ulti-mately receives salvation; and the man who builds with only bad materials loses his salvation. This continuum refutes the Protestant argument that the man in verse 15 is losing rewards but not incurring punishments. It also parallels Jesus' teaching in Luke 12:47–48, where the ignorant and lazy servants are punished temporally after their earthly life, while the wicked servant is punished eternally.

Because the fire consumes the bad materials used by the man in verse 15, his temple is destroyed to some degree. However, the man in verse 17 who builds with only bad materials destroys his temple completely.[206] Both men build

---

205. The Greek transliteration for "destroy" (*phtheiro*) is used six other times in the New Testament. On four of these occasions, the word refers to a corruption that results from mortal sin (2 Cor 11:3; Eph 4:22; Jude 10; Rev 19:2). Hence, when Paul uses "destroy" in 1 Cor 3:17, he is referring to the ultimate corruption that results from mortal sin: eternal damnation.

206. Paul's metaphor of bad materials and eternal destruction follows Ezekiel's prophecy in chapter 13. Ezekiel explains how the Jews built a wall on a "foundation" with "untempered mortar" (vv. 14–15; DR). Because the Jews built with faulty materials (like the wood, hay and stubble of 1 Corinthians 3), God sent His "wrath to consume" the structure (v. 13; DR). It is interesting to note how Paul refers the Corinthians to the warnings in the

with flammable materials, but the man in verse 15 was saved and the man in verse 17 was condemned. Why? It is because the man's spiritual edifice in verse 15 included fire-proof materials as well. These materials (good works) would have included confessing his sins and living a life of charity. The man in verse 17 failed to confess his sins and died unrepentant. In short, the difference between the man in verse 15 and the man in verse 17 is that the former died in a state of grace and the latter died in a state of mortal sin.

Thus, Paul's teaching in 1 Corinthians 3:14–17 reveals the three possible conditions of a person's soul at death:

> The state of perfect righteousness
> (*verse 14—the man receives the reward*).

> The state of venial sin/debt of punishment
> (*verse 15—the man suffers loss but is still saved*).

> The state of mortal sin
> (*verse 17—the man is destroyed*).

Two Classes of People?

To get around the obvious continuity of the metaphor, some Protestant apologists try to drive yet another wedge between the saved people in verses 14–15 (who did good works) and the condemned people in verse 17 (who did bad works). Artificially creating two categories of people (the saved and the damned), the Protestant apologist insists that God is punishing those who did bad works and rewarding (but not punishing) those who did good works. Like their false distinction between bad motives and sins, this

---

Old Testament about eternal damnation after he uses a similar metaphor as that used by Ezekiel (1 Cor 10:6–11).

categorization is another anachronistic (and redundant) form of argumentation.

We have already demonstrated, through an analysis of the original Greek and Hebrew, that in verse 15 God is punishing the people He ultimately saves. Further, if verses 14–15 were about rewards only and not salvation proper, then there would be nothing about condemnation in verse 17, for condemnation would be completely out of context. As it stands, Paul is referring to exactly the same types of sins (false wisdom and divisive allegiances) both before and after 1 Corinthians 3:15, which means he is speaking to the same people in verses 14–15 and verse 17.[207] These sins, which apply to all the Corinthians, destroy the temple of God partially and, if sufficiently egregious, completely.

Not only does Paul fail to make a distinction between the saved and unsaved, Paul doesn't make any distinctions among the Corinthians at all. Paul opens his letter by stating that he is writing "To the church of God which is at Corinth." (1:2). These are the same people whom Paul says has received "spiritual gifts"[208] and whom he exhorts to "build up the church,"[209] promising that their "labor is not in vain." (1 Cor 15:58). Most critically, Paul brackets his teaching in 1 Corinthians 3:14–17 by calling the Corinthians "God's building" in verse 9 and "God's temple" in verse 17, two metaphors representing the same thing—the Corinthian people.[210] These statements are bookends to Paul's "judgment

---

207. Paul emphasizes the sins of false wisdom in 1 Cor 1:20–2:9 and divisive allegiances in 1 Cor 1:10–12. Then, after his teaching in 1 Cor 3:14–17, he mentions the same sins of false wisdom in 1 Cor 3:18–20 and divisive allegiances in 1 Cor 3:21–23.

208. Cf. 1 Cor 12–14.

209. 1 Cor 14:12, 26.

210. It is true that Paul changes the metaphor from "building" to "temple" but, as we have mentioned, Paul does this to emphasize the holiness that is at

by fire" metaphor. This means the metaphor applies equally to all of the Corinthians, without distinction.[211]

Thus, God is punishing the men (in verses 15 and 17) who performed evil deeds. The difference is that the punishment in verse 15 is less severe than in verse 17 because the man in verse 15 is saved (though purged by fire) and the man in verse 17 is damned (consumed by fire). The man in verse 15 is like the ignorant and lazy servants who received beatings but live, and the man in verse 17 is like the wicked servant who is condemned. Paul's teaching emphasizes that all deeds, both good and evil, are brought to the judgment seat of Christ, for "he will render to every man according to his works." (Rom 2:6). The good deeds of the saved follow them into heaven, and the bad deeds of the damned torment them in hell.[212]

In the end, Scripture never makes a distinction among the methods God uses to judge the sinner's good and bad deeds, for all deeds will be "revealed and tested with fire." (1 Cor 3:13). As Isaiah reveals, our "filth" is "washed away" by "a spirit of judgment and by a spirit of burning" (4:4) and "the Lord shall judge by fire." (66:16). Instead, the focus of Scriptures is on the outcome of God's judgment. This, as we

---

issue. This change in metaphor does not create a new class of Christians. Jesus Christ is the "foundation" of the building (1 Cor 3:11), but Jesus is also the foundation of the "temple" as well (Mt 26:61; Mk 14:58; 15:29; Jn 2:19–21).

211. Some Protestant apologists have gone so far as to argue 1 Corinthians 3:14–17 applies only to Christian "ministers," even though the passage says nothing about "ministers" as Paul is clearly writing to the entire Corinthian church. Because purgatory involves the judgment of all people, the Protestant apologist thinks he moves the passage away from a judgment scenario to a rewards scenario by focusing solely on Christian "ministers" (even though Christian "ministers" are also subject to God's judgment and the possibility of purgatory).

212. We have also seen how the bad deeds of those who go to purgatory may also be a means of their temporal punishments.

have seen, means either destruction or reward (with a possible sojourn in purgatory).

We finish our analysis about "suffering loss" looking at
how other Scripture verses also connect "suffering" with
statements about God's "tests," "trials," and "fire" prior
to witnessing the "revelation of Christ" and receiving the
"crown of life." These examples further support that the
"test" God imposes upon the soul at death in 1 Corinthians 3
results in suffering (not loss of rewards) before one receives
eternal salvation:

> In this you rejoice, though now for a little while
> you may have to suffer various trials, so that the
> genuineness of your faith, more precious than
> gold which though perishable is tested by fire, may
> redound to praise and glory and honor at the rev-
> elation of Jesus Christ. (1 Pet 1:6–7).

> Beloved, do not be surprised at the fiery ordeal
> which comes upon you to prove you, as though
> something strange were happening to you. But
> rejoice in so far as you share Christ's sufferings,
> that you may also rejoice and be glad when his
> glory is revealed." (1 Pet 4:12–13).

> Blessed is the man who endures trial, for when he
> has stood the test he will receive the crown of life
> which God has promised to those who love him.
> (Jas 1:12).

> Do not fear what you are about to suffer. Behold,
> the devil is about to throw some of you into prison,
> that you may be tested, and for ten days you will

have tribulation. Be faithful unto death, and I will give you the crown of life.²¹³

Therefore I counsel you to buy from me gold refined by fire, that you may be rich, and white garments to clothe you and to keep the shame of your nakedness from being seen, and salve to anoint your eyes, that you may see. Those whom I love, I reprove and chasten; so be zealous and repent. (Rev 3:18–19).

The Book of Wisdom provides a beautiful scriptural account of the truth of purgatory.²¹⁴ In the following passage, notice how the sacred author incorporates the various facets of purgatory revealed in the New Testament: departed souls are tested, punished and disciplined for a time, like gold in the furnace is tried by fire, but these souls are at peace because they will receive immortality. Notice also how these souls run like "sparks through the stubble" which is a clear precedent for Paul's metaphor of "fire" burning "stubble":

But the souls of the righteous are in the hand of God, and no torment will ever touch them. In the eyes of the foolish they seemed to have died, and their departure was thought to be an afflic-tion, and their going from us to be their destruc-tion; but they are at peace. For though in the sight of men they were punished, their hope is full of immortality. Having been disciplined a little, they will receive great good, because God tested them

---

213. Rev 2:10. See also Ps 66:10; Isa 48:10; Jer 9:7; Dan 12:10; Zech 13:9; Mal 3:2–3.
214. This is the main reason why Martin Luther removed the Book of Wisdom from the canon of Scripture, even though it had been a part of the Christian Bible for previous 1500 years.

and found them worthy of himself; like gold in the furnace he tried them, and like a sacrificial burnt offering he accepted them. In the time of their visitation they will shine forth, and will run like sparks through the stubble. (3:1–7).

1 Corinthians 15:28–29: Baptism on Behalf of the Dead

In chapter 15 of the same First Letter to the Corinthians, Paul makes a much subtler allusion to the condition of departed souls. In this chapter, Paul's focus is primarily on the resurrection of the dead, but he brings purgatory into his teaching in the applicable verses. Paul begins the chapter by affirming the resurrection of Christ. Then he states that the risen Christ appeared to Peter and the apostles and thereafter to five hundred people at once, before appearing to him, adding that if Christ were not raised from the dead, then the gospel is a fraud and our faith is in vain.

After affirming the doctrine of Original Sin and the redemption, Paul speaks of "the end" where Christ will destroy the powers of darkness and the Father will subject all of Christ's enemies to His reign. Then, beginning in verse 28, Paul makes a curious statement about "the dead":

When all things are subjected to him, then the Son himself will also be subjected to him who put all things under him, that God may be everything to every one. Otherwise, what do people mean by being baptized on behalf of the dead? If the dead are not raised at all, why are people baptized on their behalf?

We first note the interesting connection between 1 Corinthians 15:24–25 and Ephesians 1:21–22, the passage we examined earlier when we looked at Matthew 12:32. Both passages reveal that Christ will conquer "every rule and power and authority" after "God has put all things in subjection under his feet."[215] We saw in Ephesians that this reign of Christ occurs "in the age to come," the same age where in Matthew Jesus says there will be "forgiveness of sin." It appears, then, that Paul has the forgiveness of sins in the afterlife on his mind, for he immediately follows his teaching about Christ's reign with references to people "being baptized on behalf of the dead." What does Paul exactly mean?

While it is not crystal clear, there are a couple of plausible interpretations. One interpretation holds that Paul was referring to the sacrament of Baptism. Some think the early Church had a practice of administering the sacrament on behalf of departed loved ones, just like the Church has always celebrated the Holy Mass on behalf of the faithful departed (we see this in the section on the writings of the Fathers). When Paul says that the church is baptizing "on behalf of" the dead, the Greek word Paul uses (*huper*) may be translated as "for the sake of," "for the benefit of," or simply "for."[216] In other words, Paul believed that the celebration of the sacrament assisted the dead. Of course, if these dead

---

215. Both 1 Cor 15:24 and Eph 1:21 use the identical Greek "*pas arche kai exousia kai dunamis,*" and both 1 Cor 15:25 and Eph 1:22 use the Greek "*hupo ho pous autos.*"

216. The Greek word *huper* is used many times throughout the New Testament and generally means "on behalf of," "for the sake of," "for the benefit of," or "for." This is almost invariably the case in the Gospels. See, for example, Mt 5:44; Mk 14:24; Lk 6:28; 9:50; 16:8; 22:19–20; Jn 6:51; 10:11, 15; 11:4, 50–52; 13:37–38; 15:13; 17:19; 18:14.

were in heaven, they'd need no assistance, and if they were in hell, they'd be unable to receive assistance. This must mean that these dead are in purgatory.

Another interpretation is that Paul was using the term "baptism" as a way to describe the various penances the Corinthians performed "on behalf of the dead."[217] The New Testament uses the word "baptism" in this way. For example, Scripture refers to the baptism of John as a "baptism for the repentance and forgiveness of sins."[218] Jesus also referred to His suffering and death as a type of "baptism."[219]

Thus, Paul could have been referring to the prayers and penitential works that the church at Corinth was offering for the dead. Whether Paul was speaking specifically of the sacrament of Baptism, or more generally of penances, cannot be known definitively, but one thing is clear: Paul believed that the works of the Corinthians would benefit the faithful departed. Again, if these dead were in heaven, they'd need no further benefit, and if they were in hell, they'd be unable to gain any benefit—therefore they must be in purgatory.

Paul's teaching in 1 Corinthians 15:29 mirrors the passage from the second Book of Maccabees, which we read in the Preface. In this passage, we see the actions of the great warrior Judas Maccabeus, who fought to preserve Judea from the corruption of the pagan world. After a bloody battle, Judas Maccabeus gathered the dead bodies of his soldiers for burial and made spiritual provisions for them. Here is the expanded passage:

---

217. A third possibility is that Paul is referring to afflictions and sufferings incurred by the Corinthians on behalf of those physically living but spiritually dead.

218. Mk 4:1; 3:3; Acts 19:4.

219. Mk 10:38–39; Lk 12:50.

So they all blessed the ways of the Lord, the righteous Judge, who reveals the things that are hidden; and they turned to prayer, beseeching that the sin which had been committed might be wholly blotted out. And the noble Judas exhorted the people to keep themselves free from sin, for they had seen with their own eyes what had happened because of the sin of those who had fallen. He also took up a collection, man by man, to the amount of two thousand drachmas of silver, and sent it to Jerusalem to provide for a sin offering. In doing this he acted very well and honorably, taking account of the resurrection. For if he were not expecting that those who had fallen would rise again, it would have been superfluous and foolish to pray for the dead. But if he was looking to the splendid reward that is laid up for those who fall asleep in godliness, it was a holy and pious thought. Therefore he made atonement for the dead, that they might be delivered from their sin. (2 Macc 12:41–45).

We see three elements in this passage that are connected to our study of purgatory. The first element is a reference to the "Judge" who is God. This is the same "Judge" of Matthew 5 who detains us in prison until we have paid the last penny, and who "reveals the things that are hidden" through the fires of His divine justice. Because of His coming judgment, the faithful Jews "turned to prayer, beseeching that the sin which had been committed might be wholly blotted out." Thus, the author puts this passage in the context of God's judgment and the forgiveness of sin.

The second element we see is Judas Maccabeus'

performing a ceremony on behalf of the dead. After exhorting the people to be free from sin, Judas takes up a financial collection and sends it to the Temple to pay for a sin
offering. A sin offering generally involved the sacrifice of a
lamb, goat, bull, or ram according to a specifically prescribed
ritual.[220] The sacrifice was offered to appease God's wrath
against the sins of Israel, and, in this case, was also considered a prayer "for the dead."

The passage closely follows 1 Corinthians 15:29 because
Judas, like the Corinthians, performs the ritual by "taking
account of the resurrection." The author says that if Judas
wasn't expecting the dead to rise again, it would have been
foolish to pray for them. Paul follows the same train of
thought when he says, "If the dead are not raised at all, why
are people baptized on their behalf?" (1 Cor 15:29).

Paul could have just as easily said, "If the Corinthians
were not expecting that those who had fallen would rise
again, it would have been superfluous and foolish to baptize
on behalf of the dead." This connection appears to be more
than coincidence, and strongly indicates that Paul had the
Maccabean passage in mind when he wrote this passage.[221]
It certainly follows that Paul viewed the Corinthians' bap-
tisms on behalf of their dead as efficacious, the same way
that Judas viewed the prayers and sin offering on behalf of
his dead. We also note that the author of Maccabees calls

---

220. Cf. Lev 4:3, 8, 14, 20–21, 24–25, 29, 32–34; 5:6–9, 11–12; 6:17, 25, 30;
　　　7:7, 37; 8:2, 14; 9:2–3, 7–8, 10, 15, 22; 10:16–17, 19; 12:6, 8; 14:13, 19, 22, 31;
　　　15:15, 30; 16:3, 5, 6, 9, 11, 25, 27; 23:19.

221. There are other similarities in these letters. For example, 2 Maccabees
　　　refers to the "expectation" of resurrection in the next life (15:44) and Paul
　　　refers to the "hope" and "fact" of resurrection in the next life (15:19–20);
　　　2 Maccabees says without the resurrection prayers for the dead would be
　　　"superfluous and foolish" (v. 44) and Paul says our faith would be "in vain"
　　　and "futile" (vv. 14,17); 2 Maccabees also refers to those who have "fallen
　　　asleep" (v. 45) and so does Paul (v. 20).

salvation the "splendid reward" just as Paul calls salvation the "reward" in 1 Corinthians 3:14.

This brings us to the third element—why these ceremonies for the dead were performed. The last verse in the passage provides the answer: that the dead "might be delivered from their sin." This verse explicitly professes a belief in purgatory, where the dead are detained in a prison beyond the grave as they pay their debt to the Judge of all men. As the last verse says, the actions of Judas (his prayers and sacrifice) were able to make "atonement for the dead." That is, Judas was able to make satisfaction for the temporal punishments the deceased were required to undergo in the afterlife (more on how we can atone for others sins in the next chapter). As we have said before, there is no need for forgiveness of sin in heaven, and no possibility of forgiveness of sin in hell. Judas was praying and making atonement for the souls in purgatory.[222]

Even if Protestants do not accept the canonicity of the books of Maccabees, they can see that purgatory is not a Catholic invention. God revealed the truth of purgatory to the Jews long before the coming of Christ. Moreover, there are other examples in the Old Testament scriptures (those that Protestants accept as canonical) of ritual prayer and penitent mourning for the dead for specific periods of time.[223] The Jews understood that these practices freed the departed souls from their painful state of purification and expedited their journey to God. This is why Naomi cried

---

222. As we mentioned in our analysis of Lazarus and the rich man, departed souls were required to expiate their sins in the abode of purgatory before Christ opened the gates of heaven with His Ascension, just as they are required to do so today.

223. E.g., Gen 50:10; Num 20:29; Deut 34:8. We also see in Zech 9:11 that God, through the blood of His covenant, "will set your captives free from the waterless pit," another likely reference to the spiritual abode of purgatory.

out, "Blessed be he by the Lord, whose kindness has not forsaken the living or the dead!" (Ruth 2:20). The Jews would perform acts of kindness for the dead to free them from their sufferings. Hence, the Book of Sirach says, "Graciously give to all the living, and withhold not kindness from the dead."[224]

2 Timothy 1:16–18:
Finding Mercy on That Day

In his second letter to Timothy, whom Paul ordained a bishop at Ephesus around A.D. 65, Paul says a lot about apostolic authority in the Church. Referring to Timothy's ordination, Paul reminds Timothy to "rekindle the gift of God that is within you through the laying on of my hands." (1:6). Paul then instructs Timothy to follow, guard, and transmit to future generations the oral Tradition that he received from Paul.[225] In addition to following oral Tradition and Paul's own example, Paul also instructs Timothy to preach the Word and use Sacred Scripture.[226] Paul further warns Timothy to be careful of evil people who disregard apostolic authority and upset the Faith.[227]

Paul's friend Onesiphorus was definitely not one of those people. While we don't know much about him, we do know that he was of great service to Paul during his missions and to the church at Ephesus. Paul writes:

---

224. 7:33. Like Sirach (Ecclesiasticus), Baruch is another book that was rejected by the Protestant "Reformers." In that book, Baruch implores God to "hear now the prayer of the dead of Israel" (3:4) which, if referring to those literally (not spiritually) dead, reveals that the souls in purgatory can also pray for us.
225. 1 Tim 1:13; 2:2.
226. 1 Tim 3:10, 14, 16–17; 4:1–2.
227. 1 Tim 1:15, 2:17, 20; 3:6–9, 4:3; 4:14.

> May the Lord grant mercy to the household of
> Onesiphorus, for he often refreshed me; he was
> not ashamed of my chains, but when he arrived in
> Rome he searched for me eagerly and found me—
> may the Lord grant him to find mercy from the
> Lord on that Day—and you well know all the ser-
> vice he rendered at Ephesus.[228]

In this passage, we once again see Paul referring to "that Day." We have already examined a number of Scripture passages that demonstrate that the "Day" refers to God's judgment on the individual soul, so there is no need to repeat the analysis here.[229] We can be particularly certain that Paul is referring to Onesiphorus's Particular Judgment because Paul uses the exact same Greek phrase, "on that Day," to describe his own Particular Judgment later in the same letter, when God will have "laid up for me the crown of righteousness."[230]

We do not know from Scripture whether Onesiphorus is dead when Paul is writing his letter. Protestants who oppose purgatory often argue that Onesiphorus is not dead because there is evidence in the historical record that he was martyred in A.D. 81 under the Emperor Domitian, years after Paul was martyred in Rome. Catholics have no objection to this assertion. Whether Onesiphorus is dead or alive is not relevant to the question of purgatory. Whether Onesiphorus's "Day" had already come is not Paul's concern. Rather, Paul's focus is on imploring God to have mercy on Onesiphorus on "that Day," whenever that Day is to come.

---

228. 2 Tim 1:16–18. See also 2 Tim 4:19 where Paul closes his letter by greeting "the household of Onesiphorus."
229. We have examined 1 Cor 1:18; 3:14; 5:5; 2 Tim 4:8; Heb 10:25.
230. 4:8. In both 2 Tim 1:18 and 4:8, Paul uses the unique Greek phrase "*en ekeinos ho hemera*" which literally means "in that The Day."

Because "that Day" refers to Onesiphorus's Particular Judgment, as we have seen from other Scriptures, why is Paul asking the Lord to have mercy on him? From a Protestant perspective, this need for mercy is particularly confusing given Onesiphorus's status in the Christian community. Onesiphorus is described as a valiant Christian minister. He often "refreshed" Paul and was not "ashamed" of imprisonment for the gospel. He also "searched eagerly" for Paul in Rome and found him, and everyone knew the great "service" he rendered at Ephesus. His martyrdom would only testify to the fact that this was a man of great grace, who persevered in faith, hope, and charity to the end of his life.

If Onesiphorus was so good, we might ask Protestants, then why would Paul ask God to have mercy on him? Wasn't Onesiphorus already saved by "faith alone," and don't his good works simply testify to his status as an already-saved Christian? Wouldn't Onesiphorus be covered with the imputed righteousness of Christ on "that Day," which would make Paul's request for mercy superfluous? Whether Onesiphorus is dead or alive, this short passage says a lot in support of the Catholic view of purgatory and salvation.

First, it says that Onesiphorus, as a "saved" Christian, could still have sinned against the Faith, which is why Paul asks God for mercy on his judgment day. In other words, Paul believes that Onesiphorus could have done something to jeopardize his salvation in the eyes of God, just as Paul believed (in 1 Corinthians 9:27) that he himself could become a reprobate. That is why Paul asks God for mercy. Secondly, Paul's prayer for mercy tells us that prayer assists Onesiphorus in the afterlife. Because it is a prayer for mercy "in that Day," it is directed at appeasing God for Onesiphorus's sins, for that is the goal of such prayers. Paul was simply following Jesus' teaching in Matthew 12:32, which says that there is forgiveness of sin in "the age to come," and that is the age of purgatory.

Hebrews 12:22–24:
Even Just Men Are "Made Perfect"

Paul's Letter to the Hebrews is one of the most theologically rich epistles in the New Testament. Paul dedicates a large part of the letter to explaining the heavenly priesthood of Jesus Christ.[231] Paul emphasizes that Jesus exercises His priesthood in the same manner as that of Melchizedek, the first priest mentioned in the Old Testament who offered a sacrifice of bread and wine.[232] In the heavenly liturgy, Jesus our High Priest presents His eternal sacrifice to the Father and through the priests of the New Covenant under the appearance of bread and wine.

In chapter 12, Paul reveals to the Hebrews that their earthly liturgy is an actual participation in the heavenly liturgy where the angels and saints worship God through the mediation of Jesus Christ and His shed blood:

> But you have come to Mount Zion and to the city of the living God, the heavenly Jerusalem, and to innumerable angels in festal gathering, and to the assembly of the first-born who are enrolled in heaven, and to a judge who is God of all, and to the spirits of just men made perfect, and to Jesus, the mediator of a new covenant, and to the sprinkled blood that speaks more graciously than the blood of Abel.

---

231. Cf. Heb 4:14; 8:1–2; 9:11–12; 10:21–22.
232. Cf. Heb 5:6, 10; 6:20; 7:15, 17.

Among those who are present at the heavenly liturgy are "the spirits of just men made perfect." Paul's use of "spirits of the just" reminds us of Peter's reference to the "spirits in prison" to whom Jesus preached the gospel during His descent into the abode of the dead.[233] Paul says that these "spirits," which exist in the eternal realm, are "made perfect." They do not necessarily arrive in eternity in perfect condition. This, of course, is because most people do not achieve spiritual perfection during their earthly lives. Thus, Paul is alluding to the "spirits" (souls) who have been "made perfect" in the "prison" of purgatory. This perfection comes about by virtue of Jesus' heavenly priesthood, which is the focus of Paul's letter.

The original language lends further support to our conclusion. The Greek transliteration for the verb "made perfect" in Hebrews 12:23 is *teleíoo*, which means to perfect something by "completing it" or "bringing it to an end." Because it is a perfect past participle (literally, "having been matured"), this verb means that these souls have been perfected prior to their arrival in "the city of the living God, the heavenly Jerusalem." Yet, because Paul is referring to the "spirits" of these perfected ones indicates that these souls were perfected after having left their bodies in death. In other words, the perfect past participle connotes that the "spirits" were perfected as spirits—that is, in eternity—and that the effects of their perfection continue in eternity. Thus, Paul's usage reveals that the spirits of these just men have been perfected beyond the grave, but before reaching heaven: which means in purgatory.

Paul uses this verb (*teleíoo*) in regard to achieving perfection eight other times in his letter to the Hebrews. In each

---

233. 1 Pet 3:19. Peter and Paul use the same Greek word *pneuma* to describe the disembodied souls.

case, the "perfection" Paul describes is either connected to "suffering"[234] or to "sacrifices."[235] It follows that the perfection of the "spirits of the just men" in Hebrews 12:23 is also connected to suffering and sacrifice—the sufferings they have endured in purgatory and the sacrifices that were offered to deliver them. In fact, at the beginning of chapter 12, Paul repeatedly refers to how God "disciplines," "punishes" and "chastises" his sons so that "we may share his holiness," which is necessary to see God.[236] Paul also refers to God, who is doing the disciplining, as "the Father of spirits." (12:9). These "spirits" in verse 9 are the same "spirits" in verse 23 who are made perfect by the Father's chastisements in eternity. Finally, chapter 12 concludes by describing God as "a consuming fire"—the very fire that perfects the "spirits of the just men" in purgatory.

The Teachings of the Church Fathers

We now turn to the writings of the early Church Fathers. We call these pioneering Christians "Fathers" because they are our spiritual fathers in the faith. They were the closest to Christ, the apostles, and the original transmission of the gospel. They were the men who wrote the first commentaries on Scripture, organized the Church's earliest councils, and helped formulate the core dogmatic teachings of Christianity that even most Protestants accept (the Trinity, the two natures and wills of Christ, the hypostatic union,

---

234. Heb 2:10; 5:9; 11:40.
235. Heb 7:19, 28; 9:9; 10:1, 14. Paul teaches that the sacrifices of the Old law could not perfect the conscience of the worshiper while the "sacrifices" of the New law can do so (Heb 9:14, 23).
236. 12:10. See also Heb 12:14. Paul refers to "discipline" eight times in seven verses (vv. 5–11), in addition to his use of "punished" (v. 5) and "chastises" (v. 6).

etc.). They also had one thing in common: they all claimed membership in the Catholic Church, "the pinnacle and bulwark of the truth." (1 Tim 3:15). That is because there was no other "church" around.

Because the writings of the Fathers pose so many problems for Protestant theology, many Protestants are quick to dismiss their writings as "extra-biblical tradition." Such a dismissal, however, is contrary to the mandate of Scripture itself. As we have mentioned, Paul commands us to obey both the written and the oral revelation which we have received from Christ and the apostles.[237] The oral revelation, which we call Sacred Tradition, has been preserved in the writings of the Church Fathers, as well as in the Church's councils, catechisms, and liturgies. God has entrusted both the oral and written revelation to the Church that Christ built upon the rock of Peter and his successors, the Roman Catholic Church. (Mt 16:18). This is why Peter says, "Scripture is not a matter of one's own interpretation." (2 Pet 1:20). Instead, Scripture is a matter of the public interpretation of the Church, to which Christ gave the authority to bind and loose. (Cf. Mt 16:19; 18:18).

Some Protestants characterize the Patristic writings as inaccurate and even fraudulent. Catholics find such charges quite curious. Protestants have no problem with putting their complete faith in Scripture, even though we do not have any of the original autographs of Scripture, but rather only copies that are replete with textual variations. One might say there is more consistency in the manuscripts of the Fathers than in Scripture itself, yet Protestants have no problem dismissing the former as unreliable but not the latter. Although Scripture is inspired by God and the writings

---

237. Cf. 2 Thess 2:15; 3:6; 1 Cor 11:2.

of the Fathers are not, the Patristic writings bear witness to the early Church's interpretation of the Scriptures, and are, historically speaking, just as authentic as the copies of the Scriptures themselves.

It is critical to note that the Church Fathers were unanimous in their belief in purgatory. Although the Fathers expressed themselves differently about the doctrine, they all believed in a place of purgation after death, which they gleaned from the Scriptures we have just examined. In fact, there is more Patristic evidence supporting the doctrine of purgatory than there is for the core dogmas of the Trinity or Christology. As we have said, the doctrine of purgatory was never seriously questioned until the Protestant theological revolt in the sixteenth century. Given the abundance of biblical and patristic support for the doctrine, it is truly remarkable how the "Reformers" set aside this perennial teaching, and how many Christians of today are unaware of these basic historical facts.

If the Protestant wishes to dismiss the writings of the Fathers on purgatory, on what basis does he accept their writings on the Trinity or the Incarnation? On what basis does he accept their writings on heaven and hell? I pose these questions to underscore the futility of the private judgment theology of Protestantism. If one wishes to dismiss the Fathers' writings, then he is either burying his head in the sand or accusing the earliest Christian leaders of falling into mass apostasy.[238] To argue that the Fathers were wrong

---

238. Many Protestants claim that the Holy Spirit guides them when interpreting Scripture. But weren't the early Church Fathers also guided by the Spirit when interpreting Scripture? It is quite arrogant for any of us twenty-first-century Westerners to claim we know better than the Fathers, particularly when they received their understanding of Scripture from the successors to the apostles, and some even from the apostles themselves (Ignatius of Antioch, Polycarp, Clement). Protestants may concede that

about purgatory is essentially to argue that Christ abandoned His Church from the beginning, even though Jesus promised that the gates of hell would not prevail against His Church. (Cf. Mt 16:18).

The unanimous interpretation of the Fathers is further supported by the inscriptions on the tombs, sepulchers, and catacombs of the first martyrs and departed faithful of the Catholic Church. In many of these inscriptions, some dating back to the first century, the deceased Christians beg for the prayers of the living. In his study of the inscriptions of many catacombs in Rome, Fr. John O'Brien saw the last words of the dying Christians: "In your prayers remember us who have gone before you."[239] These inscriptions reveal the early Church's belief in purgatory and the efficacy of prayers to assist the dead. Father A.S. Barnes has compiled many of these inscriptions from the first three centuries of the Church in his book *The Early Church in the Light of the Monuments.*[240]

The earliest liturgies of the Church also reflect a belief in purgatory. From the very beginning, the Church in the Holy Mass would remember the faithful departed, with prayers for their peace and the forgiveness of their sins. One of the oldest liturgies, attributed to the Apostle James, contains the prayer, "We commemorate all the faithful dead who have died in the true faith . . . We ask, we entreat, we pray Christ our God, who took their souls and spirits to Himself, that by His many compassions He will make them worthy of

---

"some" Fathers were guided by the Spirit, but not all of them. The problem with that argument is that all of the Fathers believed in purgatory! Either the early Church became apostate by believing in purgatory, or those who reject purgatory are rejecting an apostolic doctrine of the Faith.

239. *The Faith of Millions* (Huntington, IN: Our Sunday Visitor, 1974), p.340.
240. *The Early Church in the Light of the Monuments* (New York: Longmans, Green & Co, 1913), pp. 149–157.

the pardon of their faults and the remission of their sins."[241]

In the fourth century, Cyril of Jerusalem expressed the Church's belief that "the souls of those for whom prayers are offered [during Mass] receive very great relief." In the Traditional Latin Mass, which was originally composed by Peter and Paul in Rome, the priest offers the sacrifice "for the living and the dead, that it may avail both me and them for salvation unto life everlasting." The priest also asks God to grant to the dead "a place of refreshment, light, and peace."

Let us now examine some of the writings of the Church Fathers, in chronological order, with some commentary along the way. You'll see that their interpretations of Scripture only echo the exegesis we have offered in this and previous chapters. Please also note that this is just a sampling of the writings of the Fathers on the topic of purgatory. I'd encourage you to consult the bibliography at the end of this chapter for further study not only about the dogma of purgatory, but also about the other core dogmas of the Catholic faith (all believed by the Fathers).

The Acts of Paul and Thecla
Early Christian Writing, c.160

And after the exhibition, Tryphaena again received her [Thecla]. For her daughter Falconilla had died, and said to her in a dream: 'Mother, you shall have this stranger Thecla in my place, in order that she may pray concerning me, and that I may be transferred to the place of the just.[242]

COMMENTARY: Here we see, in the second century, the early Christians' belief in a state in the afterlife that is neither heaven nor hell. The

241. Syriac Liturgy of St. James, "Prayers for the Dead," *Catholic Encyclopedia* (1908).
242. *Acts of Paul and Thecla* (A.D. 160).

departed Falconilla reveals to her mother Tryphaena that she is in purgatory and that Thecla's prayers can assist her. Through Thecla's prayers, Falconilla knows that she will be "transferred" from purgatory to heaven, the "place of the just."

Abercius
Bishop of Hierpolis, d.167

The citizen of a prominent city, I erected this while I lived, that I might have a resting place for my body. Abercius is my name, a disciple of the chaste Shepherd who feeds his sheep on the mountains and in the fields, who has great eyes surveying everywhere, who taught me the faithful writings of life. Standing by, I, Abercius, ordered this to be inscribed: Truly, I was in the course of my seventy-second year. May everyone who is in accord with this and who understands it pray for Abercius. *Inscription of Abercius (A.D. 190)*

COMMENTARY: This is another second-century example of the early Christians' belief in purgatory. Abercius inscribed on his epitaph a request for prayers for his soul. All Christians believed that these prayers could assist the dead by helping to make satisfaction for the sins that detained them in purgatory.

The Martyrdom of Perpetua and Felicity
Early Christian Martyrs at Carthage, d.203

Without delay, on that very night, this was shown to me in a vision: I [Perpetua] saw Dinocrates going out from a gloomy place, where also there were several others, and he was parched and very thirsty, with a filthy countenance and pallid color, and the wound on his face which he had when he died. This Dinocrates had been my brother after the flesh, seven years of age, who died miserably with disease . . . For him I had made my prayer, and between him and me there was a large interval, so that neither of us could approach to the other . . . and [I] knew that my brother was in suffering. But I trusted that my prayer would bring help to his suffering; and I prayed for him every day until we passed over into the prison of the camp, for we were to fight in the camp-show. Then . . . I made my prayer for my brother day and night, groaning and weeping that he might be granted to me.

Then, on the day on which we remained in fetters, this was shown to me: I saw that that place which I had formerly observed to be in gloom was now bright; and Dinocrates, with a clean body well clad, was finding refreshment. And where there had been a wound, I saw a scar; and that pool which I had before seen, I saw now with its margin lowered even to the boy's navel. And one drew water from the pool incessantly, and upon its brink was a goblet filled with water; and Dinocrates drew near and began to drink from it, and the goblet did not fail. And when he was satisfied, he went away from the water to play joyously, after the manner of children, and I awoke. Then I understood that he was translated from the place of punishment. *The Martyrdom of Perpetua and Felicitias (A.D. 203)*

COMMENTARY: In this vision, Perpetua sees her deceased brother Dinocrates suffering the torments of purgatory. Perpetua even describes it as the "the place of punishment." Dinocrates was parched and thirsty with a filthy and wounded appearance. Perpetua also reveals that a large chasm separated her from her brother, just as Lazarus was separated from the rich man in Luke 16:26. Perpetua also expresses confidence that her prayers would "bring help to his suffering." Perpetua seems to allude to the process of Dinocrates's purification when she says his appearance had changed and he was finding refreshment. In the end, Perpetua reveals that Dinocrates was "translated" from his punishments to a state of joy.

Clement of Alexandria
Theologian, d.215

Accordingly the believer, through great discipline, divesting himself of the passions, passes to the mansion which is better than the former one, viz., to the greatest torment, taking with him the characteristic of repentance from the sins he *has* committed after baptism. He is tortured then still more—not yet or not quite attaining what he sees others to have acquired. Besides, he is also ashamed of his transgressions. The greatest torments, indeed, are assigned to the believer. For God's righteousness is good, and His goodness is righteous. And though the punishments cease in the course of the completion of the expiation and purification of each one, yet those have very great and permanent grief who are found worthy of the other fold, on account of not being along with those that have been glorified through righteousness." *Stromata, 6:14 (ante A.D. 202)*

COMMENTARY: Clement is writing about the pains of purgatory, which he describes as "torture" for the "sins" (works, deeds, bad materials) the departed committed during his lifetime. Clement is clear that these post-death sufferings are temporal and not eternal, for they cease after the expiation of sin is completed, and then the person passes to the "better mansion."

Tertullian
Theologian, d. c.225

"[T]hat allegory of the Lord which is extremely clear and simple in its meaning, and ought to be from the first understood in its plain and natural sense . . . Then, again, should you be disposed to apply the term "adversary" to the devil, you are advised by the [Lord's] injunction, while you are in the way with him, to make even with him such a compact as may be deemed compatible with the requirements of your true faith. Now the compact you have made respecting him is to renounce him, and his pomp, and his angels. Such is your agreement in this matter. Now the friendly understanding you will have to carry out must arise from your observance of the compact: you must never think of getting back any of the things which you have abjured, and have restored to him, lest he should summon you as a fraudulent man, and a transgressor of your agreement, before God the Judge (for in this light do we read of him, in another passage, as "the accuser of the brethren," or saints, where reference is made to the actual practice of legal prosecution); and lest this Judge deliver you over to the angel who is to execute the sentence, and he commit you to the prison of hell, out of which there will be no dismissal until the smallest even of your delinquencies be paid off in the period before the resurrection. What can be a more fitting sense than this? What a truer interpretation? *A Treatise on the Soul, 35 (A.D. 210)*

COMMENTARY: Tertullian provides us with the earliest interpretation of Matthew 5:25–26, which he deems to be clear, simple, and self-evident. As we saw earlier, the "accuser" is the devil, whom we are to renounce in this life. If we fail to do so, the Judge will hand us over to an angel who will confine us to the "prison" of hell (Hades) where we will make satisfaction for even our smallest faults. It is clear that this post-mortem place of detention is not the eternal hell of the reprobate, for there will be "dismissal" after the delinquencies are satisfied.

All souls, therefore, are shut up within Hades: do you admit this? [It is true, whether] you say yes or no: moreover, there are already experienced there punishments and consolations; and there you have a poor man and a rich . . . Moreover, the soul executes not all its operations with the ministration of the flesh; for the judgment of God pursues even simple cogitations and the merest volitions. "Whosoever looks on a woman to lust after her, has committed adultery with her already in his heart." Therefore, even for this cause it is most fitting that the soul, without at all waiting for the flesh, should be punished for what it has done without the partnership of the flesh. So, on the same principle, in return for the pious and kindly thoughts in which it shared not the help of the flesh, shall it without the flesh receive its consolation. In short, inasmuch as we understand "the prison" pointed out in the Gospel to be Hades, and as we also interpret "the uttermost farthing" [the last penny] to mean the very smallest offense which has to be recompensed there before the resurrection, no one will hesitate to believe that the soul undergoes in Hades some compensatory discipline, without prejudice to the full process of the resurrection, when the recompense will be administered through the flesh besides. *A Treatise on the Soul, 58 (A.D. 210)*

COMMENTARY: Tertullian seems to believe the rich man of Luke 16 is in purgatory (which he calls Hades) because the rich man (often referred to as "Dives") is with him. Note how he focuses on God's judgment of the individual soul and how the soul is punished after death for even mental infractions (lust). This emphasizes how God looks into the soul of man as He judges him, and not to an imputed righteousness that covers the soul. He also interprets Matthew 5:25–26 to be about purgatory and emphasizes that the soul is caused to make satisfaction for the sins committed in the body which is represented by the payment of debt.

As often as the anniversary comes round, we make offerings for the dead as birthday honors. *The Chaplut, 3 (A.D. 211)*

COMMENTARY: Tertullian acknowledges the Church's perennial custom of offering sacrifices (that is, the Eucharistic sacrifice) for the dead, just as Judas Maccabeus offered a sacrifice for the dead. Since the very beginning, the Church would make offerings for the dead to loose them from their sins.

[A] woman is more bound when her husband is dead. ... Indeed, she prays for his soul, and requests refreshment for him ... and fellowship with him in the first resurrection; and she offers the sacrifice on the anniversary of his falling asleep. *On Monogamy, 10 (A.D. 216)*

COMMENTARY: Tertullian is clear that the Christian prays and offers sacrifice for the souls of departed loved ones. There is no need to offer prayers for those in heaven or hell, which means these prayers are for the souls in purgatory.

Origen
Theologian, d.254

For if on the foundation of Christ you have built not only gold and silver and precious stones, but also wood and hay and stubble, what do you expect when the soul shall be separated from the body? Would you enter into heaven with your wood and hay and stubble and thus defile the kingdom of God; or on account of these hindrances would you remain without and receive no reward for your gold and silver and precious stones; neither is this just. It remains then that you be committed to the fire which will burn the light materials, for our God to those who can comprehend heavenly things is called a cleansing fire. But this fire consumes not the creature, but what the creature has himself built, wood, and hay and stubble. It is manifest that the fire destroys the wood of our transgressions and then returns to us the reward of our great works. *Homilies on Jeremiah, PG 13:445, 448 (A.D. 244)*

COMMENTARY: Origen interprets 1 Corinthians 3:14–15 to be a revelation of purgatory, and holds that purgatory is necessary as a matter of justice. He equates the wood, hay, and stubble with our "transgressions" (sins), which God purges with His "cleansing fire." It is only after the purgation is completed that the soul receives its reward.

Cyprian of Carthage
Bishop and Martyr, d.258

It is one thing to stand for pardon, another thing to attain to glory: it is one thing, when cast into prison, not to go out thence until one has paid the uttermost farthing [last penny]; another thing at once to receive the wages of faith and courage. It is one thing, tortured by long suffering for sins, to be cleansed and long purged by fire; another to have purged all sins by suffering. It is one thing, in fine, to be in suspense till the sentence of God at the day of judgment; another to be at once crowned by the Lord. *To Antonianus, Epistle 51 (55):20 (A.D. 253)*

COMMENTARY: Cyprian is speaking about the difference between gaining heaven immediately and having to go to purgatory first. He equates purgatory with "pardon," which means venial (not mortal) sin is forgiven. He also interprets Matthew 5:25–26 to be an allusion to purgatory when he references the "prison" and payment of the last "farthing." He further describes purgatory as "torture" and "suffering" for "sin" through purgation by "fire."

Apostolic Constitutions
Early Collection of Christian writings, c.350

Let us pray for our brethren that are at rest in Christ, that God, the lover of mankind, who has received his soul, may forgive him every sin, voluntary and involuntary, and may be merciful and gracious to him, and give him his lot in the land of the pious that are sent into the bosom of Abraham, and Isaac, and Jacob, with all those that have pleased Him and done His will from the beginning of the world, whence all sorrow, grief, and lamentation are banished. *Apostolic Constitutions, 8:4,41*

COMMENTARY: This passage clearly demonstrates the early Church's belief in purgatory. The author exhorts us to pray for the souls of the dead that they may be forgiven of sin. The author's reference to "involuntary" sin refers to the dispositions of the soul and a failure to master concupiscence.

Lactantius
Theologian, d.325

The same divine fire, therefore, with one and the same force and power, will both burn the wicked and will form them again, and will replace as much as it shall consume of their bodies, and will supply itself with eternal nourishment: which the poets transferred to the vulture of Tityus. Thus, without any wasting of bodies, which regain their substance, it will only burn and affect them with a sense of pain. But when He shall have judged the righteous, He will also try them with fire. Then they whose sins shall exceed either in weight or in number, shall be scorched by the fire and burnt:

but they whom full justice and maturity of virtue has imbued will not perceive that fire; for they have something of God in themselves which repels and rejects the violence of the flame. *The Divine Institutes, 7:21 (A.D. 307)*

COMMENTARY: Lactantius indicates that the fires of hell and purgatory are the same, but with different effects—the former consumes and the latter purges. He is clear that the righteous are tried by fire after their death on account of their sins. He also notes that those who have reached perfection are not burned by the fire. This is consistent with 1 Corinthians 3:15—the man must pass through the fire only if he has built with faulty materials.

Cyril of Jerusalem

Bishop and Doctor of the Church, d.386

Then we commemorate also those who have fallen asleep before us: first, the patriarchs, prophets, apostles, and martyrs, that at their prayers and intercessions God would receive our petition. Then on behalf also of the holy Fathers and bishops who have fallen asleep before us, and in a word of all who in past years have fallen asleep among us, believing that it will be a very great benefit to the souls, for whom the supplication is put up, while that holy and most awful sacrifice is set forth. And I wish to persuade you by an illustration. For I know that many say, what is a soul profited, which departs from this world either with sins, or without sins, if it be commemorated in the prayer? For if a king were to banish certain who had given him offense, and then those who belong to them should weave a crown and offer it to him on behalf of those under punishment, would he not grant a remission of their penalties? In the same way we, when we offer to Him our supplications for those who have fallen asleep, though they be sinners, weave no crown, but offer up Christ sacrificed for our sins, propitiating our merciful God for them as well as for ourselves. *Catechetical Lectures, 23:9, 10 (c. A.D. 350)*

COMMENTARY: Cyril explains that Christians pray for the dead (those who have "fallen asleep") and that these prayers are beneficial to the departed souls because of their sins. He also likens the condition of the departed souls to those who suffer "punishment" and "penalties" under the direction of a king (an allusion to Christ). He further mentions the chief of all prayers for the dead, the Holy Sacrifice of the Mass (the "most awful sacrifice") where Christ is "sacrificed for our sins" to "propitiate" God's wrath.

Basil
Bishop and Doctor of the Church, d.379

I think that the noble athletes of God, who have wrestled all their lives with the invisible enemies, after they have escaped all of their persecutions and have come to the end of life, are examined by the prince of this world and, if they are found to have any wounds from their wrestling, any stains or effects of sin, they are detained. If, however, they are found unwounded and without stain, they are, as unconquered, brought by Christ into their rest. *Homilies on the Psalms, 7:2 (ante A.D. 370)*

COMMENTARY: Basil describes what happens to those who die with either the stain of sin ("unconquered" concupiscence) or the effects of sin (the debts of temporal punishment). If souls are found with these wounds at the judgment, they are "detained," which is a clear reference to the "prison" of Matthew 5:25–26. If souls are found without these wounds (they built only with gold, silver, precious stones), then they immediately enter heaven.

Ephraem
Theologian, d.373

Lay me not with sweet spices, for this honor avails me not; Nor yet incense and perfumes, for the honor benefits me not. Burn sweet spices in the Holy Place, and me, even me, conduct to the grave with prayer. Give incense to God and over me send up hymns. Instead of perfumes of spices, in prayer make remembrance of me. *His Testament (ante A.D. 373)*

COMMENTARY: Ephraem emphasizes the importance of prayer and offerings for the benefit of his departed soul. He values prayer more than the honors traditionally bestowed on the deceased (spices, incense, perfumes). We repeat ourselves again: prayer is unnecessary for the souls in heaven, and ineffective to help the souls in hell.

Epiphanius
Bishop and Monk, d.403

Useful too is the prayer fashioned on their behalf [of the dead], even if it does not force back the whole of guilty charges laid to them. And it is useful also, because in this world we often stumble either voluntarily or involuntarily, and thus it is a reminder to do better. *Panarion, 75:8 (A.D. 375)*

COMMENTARY: Epiphanius confirms the early Church's practice of praying for the dead, which makes satisfaction for some, if not all, of the guilt of their sins. He also alludes to the internal dimension of sin ("voluntary" through deeds or "involuntary" through concupiscence) which bears upon whether or not we will suffer in purgatory. Praying for the dead is "useful" not only for the departed, but for the living as well, because it reminds us to do good in this life so that we don't have to suffer in the next life.

Gregory of Nyssa
Bishop, d. c.395

If a man distinguish in himself what is peculiarly human from that which is irrational, and if he be on the watch for a life of greater urbanity for himself, in this present life he will purify himself of any evil contracted, overcoming the irrational by reason. If he has inclined to the irrational pressure of the passions, using for the passions the cooperating hide of things irrational, he may afterward in a quite different manner be very much interested in what is better, when, after his departure out of the body, he gains knowledge of the difference between virtue and vice and finds that he is not able to partake of divinity until he has been purged of the filthy contagion in his soul by the purifying fire. *Sermon on the Dead*, PG 13:445, 448 (ante A.D. 394)

COMMENTARY: Gregory emphasizes the tension between the spirit and the flesh, between reason and the passions. He teaches that giving in to the temptations of the passions causes a "filthy contagion in his soul" which we have referred to as the stain or remnants of sin. Gregory is clear that this defilement of soul must be "purged" in the "purifying fire" after death before one can be admitted to heaven. He also indicates that we would rather suffer in this life by overcoming these weaknesses than be purged of them by fire in the next life.

Ambrose
Bishop and Doctor of the Church, d.397

Blessed shall both of you be [departed Gratian
and Valentinian], if my prayers can avail anything.
No day shall pass you over in silence. No prayer
of mine shall omit to honor you. No night shall
hurry by without bestowing on you a mention in
my prayers. In every one of the oblations will I
remember you. De obitu Valent (A.D. 387)

COMMENTARY: Ambrose follows the apostolic practice of the Church in
offering prayers and oblations (the Sacrifice of the Mass) for the dead,
this time for deceased Roman emperors Valentinian and Gratian. These
prayers are not merely to honor the dead, but also to free them from their
sins, which is why they are offered in union with "the oblations."

Give, Oh Lord, rest to your servant Theodosius,
that rest you have prepared for your saints . . . I
love him, therefore will I follow him to the land
of the living; I will not leave him till by my prayers
and lamentations he shall be admitted unto the
holy mount of the Lord, to which his deserts call
him. De obitu Theodosii, PL 16:1397 (A.D. 395)

COMMENTARY: Ambrose calls his deceased friend Theodosius a "servant" of God who is among God's "saints." Yet, Ambrose believes that
Theodosius has not yet made it to heaven. Of course, Theodosius would
have been immediately admitted to heaven if he were covered with Christ's
righteousness at his Particular Judgment. Instead, it is by Ambrose's
prayers and sufferings that Theodosius will be admitted into the house
of the Lord.

Jerome
Confessor and Doctor of the Church d. 420

Other husbands scatter on the graves of their wives violets, roses, lilies, and purple flowers; and assuage the grief of their hearts by fulfilling this tender duty. Our dear Pammachius also waters the holy ashes and the revered bones of Paulina, but it is with the balm of almsgiving. *To Pammachius, Epistle 66:5 (A.D. 397)*

COMMENTARY: Jerome reveals the early Church's practice of honoring the dead. This practice includes revering the remains (bones, hair, clothing) of the holy faithful departed, which the Church calls "relics." Jerome also reveals that Pammachius assists the soul of Paulina with "almsgiving." As we will see in the next chapter, almsgiving, like prayer, is a principle way in which we are able to make satisfaction for the sins of the members of Christ's body, which includes the souls in purgatory.

John Chrysostom
Bishop and Doctor of the Church, d. 407

Mourn for those who have died in wealth, and did not from their wealth think of any solace for their soul, who had power to wash away their sins and would not. Let us all weep for these in private and in public, but with propriety, with gravity, not so as to make exhibitions of ourselves; let us weep for these, not one day, or two, but all our life. Such tears spring not from senseless passion, but from true affection. The other sort are of senseless passion. For this cause they are quickly quenched, whereas if they spring from the fear of God, they always abide with us. Let us weep for these; let us assist them according to our power; let us think of some assistance for them, small though it be, yet still let us assist them. How and in what way? By praying and entreating others to make prayers for them, by continually giving to the poor on their behalf. *Homilies on Philippians, 3 (ante A.D. 404)*

COMMENTARY: Chrysostom is speaking of the departed souls who need our intercession. He first mentions those who have died without sufficiently washing away their sins. He then says we must weep for them and assist them all the days of our life, according to our abilities. Chrysostom says that this assistance includes prayer and, like Jerome, giving alms to the poor. Through these penances, we are able to help free the dead from the sins they failed to "wash away" during their lives.

Monica
Mother of Augustine, d.387

Lay this body anywhere; let not the care of it in any way disturb you. This only I request of you, that you would remember me at the altar of the Lord, wherever you be. *Augustine's Confessions (A.D. 397)*

COMMENTARY: In this request to her son Augustine, Monica professes the apostolic Faith of the Church. She beseeches Augustine, a priest of God, to remember her soul during the Sacrifice of the Mass. This request reflects Monica's belief in purgatory.

Augustine
Bishop and Doctor of the Church, d.430

I, therefore, O God of my heart, do now beseech you for the sins of my mother. Hear me through the medicine of the wounds that hung upon the wood . . . May she, then, be in peace with her

husband . . . And inspire, my Lord . . . your servants, my brethren, whom with voice and heart
and pen I serve, that as many as shall read these
words, may remember at your altar, Monica, your
servant. *Confessions (A.D. 397)*

COMMENTARY: In this touching prayer, Augustine responds to his mother's request by imploring the Lord to forgive his mother's sins after her
death. Even though Monica faithfully served God all her life (including
praying thirty years for the conversion of her son), Augustine does not
believe that her sins were completely washed away by "faith alone" or that
her soul was "covered" with Christ's righteousness. He, like his mother,
believed in the Church's dogma of purgatory.

There is an ecclesiastical discipline, as the faithful know, when the names of the martyrs are read
aloud in that place at the altar of God, where
prayer is not offered for them. Prayer, however,
is offered for other dead who are remembered.
It is wrong to pray for a martyr, to whose prayers
we ought ourselves be commended. *Sermons 159:1
(A.D. 411)*

COMMENTARY: Augustine affirms the Church's practice of praying for the
dead at the Holy Sacrifice of the Mass. The sacrifice of the Mass, which
renews Christ's sacrifice on Calvary, satisfies God's justice, and God
responds by forgiving the sins of the faithful departed (more on the Mass
in the next chapter). Augustine also affirms the Church's belief of praying
to the saints in heaven (here, the martyrs).

But by the prayers of the holy Church, and by the
salvific sacrifice, and by the alms which are given
for their spirits, there is no doubt that the dead
are aided, that the Lord might deal more mercifully with them than their sins would deserve. The

whole Church observes this practice which was handed down by the Fathers: that it prays for those who have died in the communion of the Body and Blood of Christ, when they are commemorated in their own place in the sacrifice itself; and the sacrifice is offered also in memory of them, on their behalf. If, then, works of mercy are celebrated for the sake of those who are being remembered, who would hesitate to recommend them, on whose behalf prayers to God are not offered in vain? It is not at all to be doubted that such prayers are of profit to the dead; but for such of them as lived before their death in a way that makes it possible for these things to be useful to them after death. *Sermons, 172:2 (A.D. 411)*

COMMENTARY: Augustine is clear that offering prayers, alms, and the Holy Mass for departed souls is the practice of the "whole Church" which was "handed down by the Fathers"; that is, which comes from the apostles themselves. He indicates that these "works of mercy" appease God so that He can forgive the sins of the departed in the afterlife. Augustine is also speaking of those dead who "died in the communion of the Body and Blood of Christ"—those who professed the Catholic faith.

That there should be some fire even after this life is not incredible, and it can be inquired into and either be discovered or left hidden whether some of the faithful may be saved, some more slowly and some more quickly in the greater or lesser degree in which they loved the good things that perish, through a certain purgatorial fire. This cannot, however, be the case of any of those of whom it is said, that they "shall not inherit the kingdom of God," unless after suitable repentance their sins be

forgiven them. *Handbook on Faith, Hope, and Charity,
18:69 (A.D. 421)*

COMMENTARY: Here Augustine affirms our exegesis of 1 Corinthians 3:15: that some of the faithful are "saved through fire" in the afterlife. He also affirms that this fiery post-death purgation is a process whereby some are saved "more slowly" or "more quickly" to the degree to which they built with faulty materials (that is, loved the things that were burned up in the fire). Augustine is clear to distinguish these purgatorial punishments from the punishments of the reprobate.

The time which interposes between the death of a man and the final resurrection holds souls in hidden retreats, accordingly as each is deserving of rest or of hardship, in view of what it merited when it was living in the flesh. Nor can it be denied that the souls of the dead find relief through the piety of their friends and relatives who are still alive, when the Sacrifice of the Mediator [Mass] is offered for them, or when alms are given in the Church. But these things are of profit to those who, when they were alive, merited that they might afterward be able to be helped by these things. There is a certain manner of living, neither so good that there is no need of these helps after death, nor yet so wicked that these helps are of no avail after death. *Handbook on Faith, Hope and Charity, 29:109 (A.D. 421)*

COMMENTARY: Augustine explains that between death and resurrection certain souls are detained ("held") to make satisfaction for the deeds they committed while in the body. He also affirms that prayer, almsgiving, and the Sacrifice of the Mass "profit" the dead. Augustine concludes by pointing out the justice of purgatory, which demands a "manner of living" that warrants neither the immediate bliss of heaven nor the eternal penalty of hell.

If the baptized person fulfills the obligations demanded of a Christian, he does well. If he does not—provided he keeps the faith, without which he would perish forever—no matter in what sin or impurity remains, he will be saved, as it were, by fire; as one who has built on the foundation, which is Christ, not gold, silver, and precious stones, but wood, hay, straw, that is, not just and chaste works but wicked and unchaste works. *Faith and Works, 1:1* (*A.D. 413*)

COMMENTARY: Augustine again asserts that certain souls are saved "by fire" in accordance with their sins. He also equates the good materials of 1 Corinthians 3:15 with "just and chaste works" and the bad materials with "wicked and unchaste works." Thus, Augustine affirms that the type of works one performs during his life will determine not only his salvation but the degree to which he "will be saved, as it were, by fire."

Now on what ground does this person pray that he may not be "rebuked in indignation, nor chastened in hot displeasure"? He speaks as if he would say unto God, "Since the things which I already suffer are many in number, I pray Thee let them suffice;" and he begins to enumerate them, by way of satisfying God; offering what he suffers now, that he may not have to suffer worse evils hereafter. *Exposition of the Psalms, 38 (37):3 (A.D. 418)*

COMMENTARY: Augustine likens the experience of purgatory to being "chastened in hot displeasure." In this exposition, Augustine explains that one may pray that God accepts his earthly sufferings as a way of making "satisfaction" for his sins so that he does not have to suffer worse punishments in the afterlife, that is, in purgatory.

For our part, we recognize that even in this life some punishments are purgatorial—not, indeed, to those whose life is none the better, but rather the worse for them, but to those who are constrained by them to amend their life. All other punishments, whether temporal or eternal, inflicted as they are on every one by divine providence, are sent either on account of past sins, or of sins presently allowed in the life, or to exercise and reveal a man's graces . . . But temporary punishments are suffered by some in this life only, by others after death, by others both now and then; but all of them before that last and strictest judgment. But of those who suffer temporary punishments after death, all are not doomed to those everlasting pains which are to follow that judgment; for to some, as we have already said, what is not remitted in this world is remitted in the next, that is, they are not punished with the eternal punishment of the world to come." *City of God, 21:13 (A.D. 426)*

COMMENTARY: Augustine explains that God sends temporal punishments to those in this life to make satisfaction for past sins as well as to reveal and perfect man's grace (like God did with Abraham). He is clear that some souls also suffer temporal punishments in the afterlife, souls who will not suffer eternal punishment. This means that some of the heaven-bound will suffer post-mortem punishments in purgatory. Augustine also reveals that these temporal punishments occur before the General Judgment.

For some of the dead, indeed, the prayer of the Church or of pious individuals is heard; but it is for those who, having been regenerated in Christ, did not spend their life so wickedly that they can be judged unworthy of such compassion, nor so well that they can be considered to have no need of it. As also, after the resurrection, there will be some of the dead to whom, after they have endured the pains proper to the spirits of the dead, mercy shall be accorded, and acquittal from the punishment of the eternal fire. For were there not some whose sins, though not remitted in this life, shall be remitted in that which is to come, it could not be truly said, "They shall not be forgiven, neither in this world, neither in that which is to come." *City of God,* 21:24 (A.D. 426)

COMMENTARY: Augustine again reiterates the justice of purgatory which he describes as "pains proper to the spirits of the dead." These are the "spirits in prison" (1 Pet 3:19) and the "spirits of the just men made perfect" in purgatory (Heb 12:23) He also equates the fires of purgatory with the fires of hell because some, after suffering in the flames, will gain "acquittal from the punishment of eternal fire." Augustine bases his interpretation of this acquittal and remission of sin in the afterlife on Matthew 12:32.

Caesar of Arles
Bishop, d.543

If we neither give thanks to God in tribulations nor redeem our own sins by good works, we shall have to remain in that purgatorian fire as long as it takes for those above-mentioned lesser sins to be consumed like wood and straw and hay. *Sermon 179 (104):2* (A.D. 542)

COMMENTARY: Caesar explains that we can make satisfaction for our sins (literally, "redeem our sins") by performing good works in this life. If we don't make sufficient satisfaction for our sins, they will be purged in the fires of purgatory like the wood, hay, and stubble of 1 Corinthians 3.

Gregory the Great
Pope and Doctor of the Church, d.604

Each one will be presented to the Judge exactly as he was when he departed this life. Yet, there must be a cleansing fire before judgment, because of some minor faults that may remain to be purged away. Does not Christ, the Truth, say that if anyone blasphemes against the Holy Spirit he shall not be forgiven "either in this world or in the world to come"? (Mt. 12:32). From this statement we learn that some sins can be forgiven in this world and some in the world to come. For, if forgiveness is refused for a particular sin, we conclude logically that it is granted for others. This must apply, as I said, to slight transgressions. *Dialogues,4:39 (A.D. 594; regn. A.D. 590–604)*

COMMENTARY: Pope Gregory affirms that God judges the condition of the soul when it leaves the body (whether it is in a state of grace or a state of sin). There is nothing about Christ's righteousness covering the soul during the judgment. Gregory also affirms that "minor faults" and "slight transgressions" (venial sins) are purged away by a "cleansing fire." Gregory further refers to Christ's statement in Matthew 12:32 that there is forgiveness in the afterlife.

As we have seen, the doctrine of purgatory is not only deeply rooted in Scripture, it is also found explicitly in the writings of the early Church Fathers. The doctrine permeated the beliefs and practices of the early Christians as seen in their liturgies and inscriptions on tombs and catacombs. The Jews before the time of Christ also believed in purgatory based on God's revelations in the Old Testament. It is truly remarkable— and unfortunate—that the "Reformers" had the temerity to set aside this article of Faith, and that Protestants are not aware of these basic historical facts.

Bibliography of Patristic Sources

The foregoing material was taken from the following sources:

Catholic Encyclopedia, 16 volumes (New York: Encyclopedia Press Inc., 1907–1914).

Confessions, trans. by J. G. Pelkington (New York: Leveright Pub. Co., 1943); Coxe, Cleveland A., ed.

The Ante-Nicene Fathers: The Writings of the Fathers down to A.D. 325, 10 volumes (Buffalo and New York, 1884–86).

Denzinger Henry, The Sources of Catholic Dogma (St. Louis: Herder, 1957).

Gibbons, James, The Faith of Our Fathers (Rockford, Illinois: Tan Books, 1876, 1980).

Jurgens, Williams, A., trans., The Faith of the Early Fathers, 3 volumes (Collegeville: Liturgical, 1970).

Ludwig Schopp and Roy J. Defarri, eds., The Fathers of the Church (Washington D.C.: CUAP, 1948).

Migne, J. P., ed., Patrologia Graeca Cursus Completus, 161 volumes. (Paris: Vives, 1857–1866).

Migne, J. P., ed., Patrologia Latina Cursus Completus, 221 volumes. (Paris: Vives, 1844–1855).

Schaff, Philip and Wace, Henry, eds., A Select Library of Nicene and Post-Nicene Fathers of the Church, 14 volumes, Series 1 and 2, (Buffalo and New York, 1886–1900).

Quasten, J. and Plumpe, J. C., eds., Ancient Christian Writers, (New York: Paulist, 1946ff).

Quasten, Johannes, Patrology, 4 vols., (Westminster: Christian Classics, 1988).

HOW TO AVOID
PURGATORY

HAVING demonstrated the reality of purgatory from
Scripture and the writings of the early Christians, we
now ask the question that logically follows: how do we avoid
purgatory? There are three ways: penances, the sacraments,
and indulgences. We examine each of these ways in this final
chapter.

Penances

We have seen that we're able assist the souls in purgatory,
as well as avoid purgatory ourselves, by making satisfaction
for sins through penance. Penance (also called "suffrages")
is the means by which we convert our hearts to God and
turn away from evil, and it's expressed in visible signs, ges-
tures, and good works. Jesus Christ explicitly commands it
when He says, "Do penance: for the kingdom of heaven is
at hand,"[243] and "Bring forth therefore fruit worthy of penance."[244] Whereas Protestants often view penance only as a

---

243. Mt 3:2 (DR); see also Mt 4:17; 11:20−21; 12:41; Mk 6:12; Lk 3:3, 8; 5:32;
    10:13; 11:32; 13:3, 5; 15:7, 10; 16:30; 17:3; 24:47 (all from DR).
244. Mt 3:8 (DR).

means of sanctifying the already-saved Christian, Jesus tells us that doing penance is necessary for salvation when He says, "unless you shall do penance, you shall all likewise perish."[245]

"Penance" is synonymous with "satisfaction." Let's briefly review what this means. When someone performs a penance, he makes satisfaction for sin by restoring equality between the offender and the one offended. In human justice, this means taking away from the offender and giving it back to the one who was offended. Although, strictly speaking, the sinner takes nothing away from God, sin deprives God the love and obedience we owe Him as a matter of justice. To restore the sinner to God, something must be taken away from the sinner, thereby giving glory to God. Thus, doing penance for sin is a penal work (which is also why the souls in purgatory "suffer loss" for their bad deeds). Penal works not only make satisfaction for past sins, but also preserve the sinner from future sins, for man does not easily fall back into sin when he has experienced the punishment associated with the sin.

Scripture plainly teaches that a person's penances makes satisfaction for his own sins. For example, David describes his penances by saying, "But as for me, when they were troublesome to me, I was clothed with haircloth. I humbled my soul with fasting; and my prayer shall be turned into my bosom."[246] David's penances of fasting, prayer, and wearing a haircloth turned to his benefit by making satisfaction for his sins and gaining merits for eternal life.

But penance also can make satisfaction for another person's sins, which is why we're able assist the souls in purgatory.

For example, when Job's three friends sin by speaking ill of God, Job does penance by offering prayers and sacrifices on their behalf. In response, God tells them, "I will accept

---

245. Lk 13:3 (DR); see also Lk 13:5 (DR).
246. Ps 34:13 (DR).

his prayer not to deal with you according to your folly." (Job 42:8). Paul likewise instructs us to make satisfaction for others' sins when he says, "We who are strong ought to bear with the failings of the weak." (Rom 15:1). Paul also says that that if a man is overtaken in any trespass (sin), we "who are spiritual should restore him in a spirit of gentleness." (Gal 6:1). Paul is reiterating the teaching of the Master who restored Peter by requiring him to make a three-fold profession of love for Jesus to make satisfaction for his three-fold denial of Him.[247] Then Paul says, "bear one another's burdens" (v. 2).[248] We bear one another's burdens by freely enduring the temporal punishments that another member of the body owes God for his sins.

How is it possible that our penances can bear the burden of another's temporal punishments? It is possible because of the Passion of Jesus Christ. We have already discussed how Jesus has atoned for the eternal penalty for sin but has allowed the temporal penalties to remain. But let us emphasize again for our Protestant friends that our penances merit favor with God only because of the propitiatory death of Jesus Christ. We are united to Christ's Passion by being members of His body through the grace of baptism. Paul says, "For by one Spirit we were all baptized into one body." (1 Cor 12:13). He also says, "We were buried therefore with him by baptism into death, so that as Christ was raised from the dead by the glory of the Father, we too might walk in newness of life." (Rom 6:4).

As members of Christ's body, we receive His grace and share in His priesthood. Peter says that God chose us "to

---

247. Cf. Jn 21:15–17.
248. One of the greatest examples in Scripture of bearing another's burden is that of Simon of Cyrene, who bore the burden of our Savior's Cross (Mt 27:32; Mk 15:21; Lk 23:26).

be a holy priesthood, to offer spiritual sacrifices acceptable to God through Jesus Christ."[249] John also says that
Christ "made us a kingdom, priests to his God and Father."
(Rev 1:6). By sharing in the priesthood of Jesus Christ, we
are able to participate in Christ's redemptive work.[250] As
Paul says, right before his teaching about purgatory, "we are
God's fellow workers."[251] The Greek for "fellow workers"
(sunergoi) literally means "synergists," which means we syner-
gize or co-operate with Christ in His work of salvation (but
only by virtue of God's grace working within us). This work
includes making satisfaction for sins so that we can save others and ourselves from the fires of purgatory. As Jude says,
we "save some, by snatching them out of the fire" (v. 23).

Members of the Body Suffer Together

This mystery of atoning for another's sins is wrapped up
in the apostolic doctrine called the Communion of Saints.
When, in the Apostles' Creed, we profess our faith in "the
communion of saints," we are declaring our belief that there
is a true communion between all of God's children, whether
they are living on earth (Church Militant), in heaven

---

249. 1 Pet 2:5. In the first part of verse 5, Peter says, "and like living stones be
yourselves built into a spiritual house . . . " This is reminiscent of Paul's
teaching about "building" with "precious stones" which is tested in the
"fire" of purgatory in 1 Corinthians 3. Thus, how we exercise the royal
priesthood will determine whether or not we will have to go to purgatory.

250. There is a distinction between the "royal priesthood" of all the baptized
(1 Pet 2:9) and the ministerial priesthood of the hierarchical Church
(Pope, bishops, priests)—both of which participate in Christ's redeeming
work in different ways.

251. 1 Cor 3:9. See also Mk 16:20; Rom 8:28; 2 Cor 6:1. As Aquinas teaches, God
wills us to be His co-workers because He wills intermediary causes to preserve the order of the universe and to communicate the dignity of causality
to men. In the mystery of predestination, human freewill actions carry out
God's eternal decrees.

(Church Triumphant), or in purgatory (Church Suffering). We are all "fellow citizens with the saints, and members of the household of God." (Eph 2:19). Not even death can divide the family of God or separate us from the love of Christ. (Rom 8:35–39). Thus, all of the baptized—whether living or dead—are in a mystical, spiritual intercommunion with each other through the Church, of which Christ is the Head and we are members.[252]

Paul speaks of this communion in 1 Corinthians 12:14–27. After explaining that we become members of Christ's body through baptism, Paul compares the Mystical Body of Christ with the human body. Using the human body as a metaphor, Paul explains that "there are many parts, yet one body." As members of the one body, there is kind of a symbiotic relationship among the various parts. The eye cannot say to the hand, "I have no need of you," nor the head to the feet, "I have no need of you." Instead, the members of the body work together, depend upon one another and care for one another. Paul concludes his teaching by saying, "If one member suffers, all suffer together; if one member is honored, all rejoice together."

With this last verse, Paul is teaching that the actions of one member affect the other members. If one suffers, the whole body suffers. If one rejoices, all rejoice. Further, if one sins, the sin causes a wound that affects the entire body. Because the sin of one member affects the entire body, the members of the affected body can repair the damage. That is, one member can make satisfaction for the sins of another, just as he can make satisfaction for his own sins (that is, the temporal debts). As we have said before, if man can make satisfaction to another man (which he can), then he can also

---

252. Cf. Eph 5:23; 1 Cor 12:12, 27.

make satisfaction to God, who is more merciful than man. Because the purpose of purgatory is to complete the satisfaction owed to God, and one member of the body can make satisfaction for another, means that the suffrages of the living can assist the souls in purgatory.

We have seen, in Colossians 1:24, how Paul says that he makes up in his sufferings what is lacking in the sufferings of Christ for the sake of His body, the Church. Because Paul's sufferings are offered for the sake of the body (the Church) means that our "spiritual sacrifices" benefit the Church at large. There is a perennial bond of charity among the members of the Church, whether on earth, in heaven, or in purgatory. This is why Paul says that "charity never ends."[253] Paul also says, "None of us lives to himself, and none of us dies to himself." (Rom 14:7). All of our acts of charity redound to the profit of all, and these acts include the penances we perform for the benefit of another.

We call these acts of charity the spiritual goods of the Communion of Saints. These spiritual goods are part of what the Church calls its "treasury." The Church's treasury is the infinite value that Christ's merits have before God the Father, along with the prayers and good works of the Blessed Virgin Mary and all the saints. Scripture, in fact, refers to the treasury as the "fine linen" that "is the righteous deeds of the saints." (Rev 19:8). In describing the early Christians, Luke says that they "were of one heart and soul, and no one said that any of the things which he possessed was his own, but they had everything in common." (Acts 4:32). The spiritual goods of the Church are held in common by all its members, so that the good works and penances of one member can benefit another. Because charity "does not insist on its own

---

253. 1 Cor 13:8 (DR).

way,"[254] we are to seek not our own good, but the good of our neighbor. (Cf. 1 Cor 10:24). We do this through the offering of penances.

Since Protestants generally acknowledge that we continue to commit sin until the end of our lives, some of them argue that our penances cannot profit the dead, for Scripture says, "We know that God does not listen to sinners." (Jn 9:31).[255] Now, it's true that God requires a person to be in a state of grace to make satisfaction for his own sins. Paul says, "if I should have all faith, so that I could remove mountains, and have not charity, I am nothing." (1 Cor 13:2). However, since we know that we receive grace according to our disposition to receive it, God measures the value of penances according to the disposition of the person for whom it is offered. If the person during his life merited to be assisted by penance after his death, God will apply the penance to the intended recipient, even if performed by one in mortal sin.

Further, Scripture says that God "makes his sun rise on the evil and on the good," which means that He can accept penances from those both in and out of grace. (Mt 5:45). The difference is that penances offered from someone in grace profit both himself and the one for whom the penance is offered, whereas penance from someone in mortal sin can benefit only the one for whom it is offered.[256]

---

254. 1 Cor 13:5.
255. Although some Protestants argue that God doesn't hear sinners (to claim that sinners cannot offer penances for the dead), those same Protestants must admit that God does hear sinners when they seek Him and repent of their sins. This shows the inconsistency of their argumentation.
256. When a person is restored to grace through repentance and confession, his previous penances performed in a state of mortal sin do not become profitable (neither meritorious for eternal life nor satisfactory for punishment). Penances performed outside of the state of grace can never be pleasing to God (see Eph 2:8–9). Nevertheless, penances done outside of grace may leave a positive effect in a person (e.g., disposing the person to do penances

Because human justice reflects Divine Justice, and one can pay another's financial debt in this life, it follows that one can pay another's spiritual debt in this life or in the next one. However, when a person makes satisfaction for another's sins, he assists in paying the sinner's debt of punishment, but not in preserving the sinner from future sins. This is because the virtuous actions of one man do not create virtue in another, except inasmuch as one man's actions may merit an increase of grace for another, which grace assists him in the preservation from future sins. It may also be the case that one who bears another's punishment does not have to undergo an equivalent punishment to make satisfaction for the sin. This is because the power of satisfaction comes from charity, and it is more charitable for one man to bear another's burdens than his own.

Also, when one makes satisfaction for the temporal punishments of another, he does not with the same penance remit the debt of his own punishments. This is because the equality of justice demands that there be a greater satisfaction offered to God for the sins of both parties than the sins of only one of them. Nevertheless, doing penance for another is still profitable for the one offering the penance. This is because, when the penitent is in a state of grace, his good works merit eternal life. As we have seen, our works are tested with fire and determine our eternal destiny. They even follow us into heaven. At the resurrection, Jesus said that "he will repay every man for what he has done"[257] and that he "will give to each of you as your works deserve."[258]

---

in grace), and this positive effect is acceptable to God.

257. Mt 16:27.

258. Rev 2:23. Penances do not profit the damned in hell because they are void of charity, nor the saints in heaven because they are perfected in charity.

The Three Forms of Penance

The three most common forms of penance by which we "bear one another's burdens" are prayer, fasting, and almsgiving. Scripture says, "Prayer is good when accompanied by fasting, almsgiving, and righteousness."[259] These three penal works correspond to the three kinds of goods that we have: bodily, spiritual, and material. Fasting deprives us of bodily goods and almsgiving deprives us of material goods. There is no need to deprive ourselves of spiritual goods because it is the state of the spirit (soul) at death that determines our eternal destiny. Yet, we perfect the spiritual life by completely submitting the bodily and material goods to our spiritual needs as a penal work. This means that we exercise the three penal works in connection with the three kinds of goods. Through the Mystical Body, these works make up for the punishment that both we and the souls in purgatory owe to God.

The Apostle John identifies the three causes of sin as "the lust of the flesh and the lust of the eyes and the pride of life." (1 Jn 2:16). In light of John's teaching, Augustine says that fasting is directed against the lust of the flesh, almsgiving against the lust of the eyes, and prayer against the pride of life. We further note that every sin injures our relationship with Christ and inflicts a wound on His body that affects both us and the other members of the body. In light of this same teaching, Aquinas says that prayer prevents us from sinning against God, almsgiving remedies sins against our neighbor, and fasting curbs sins against ourselves. Let's take a more detailed look at prayer, fasting, and almsgiving in the context of purgatory.

---

259. Tob 12:8.

1. Prayer

We have already seen many examples in Scripture where prayers are offered to benefit the dead.[260] We have also seen how the Church Fathers believed in offering prayers for the Holy Souls. There are other examples in Scripture that reveal the connection between the prayers of the living and their effects on the dead. For example, when Saul was king he sought communion with the dead. (Cf. 1 Sam 28:8–20). In response, the deceased prophet Samuel appeared to Saul and warned him of God's coming judgment.

We note that Samuel was in Abraham's bosom—the abode of the dead that was neither heaven nor hell. Nevertheless, Saul's prayer reached and had an effect on Samuel, by "bringing him up" from his temporary, post-mortem dwelling place. This is a precedent for how prayers of the living can "bring up" souls from purgatory to heaven.[261]

At His Transfiguration, Jesus communicated with Moses and Elijah, who were living in the realm of the dead.[262] When Jesus cried out on the Cross, many people thought He was summoning deceased Elijah for assistance.[263] When Jesus died, many souls were raised out of their graves and went into the city appearing to many people.[264] In the Book of Revelation, we see the prayers of those on earth ascend

---

260. 2 Macc 12:41–45; Bar 3:4; Gen 50:10; Num 20:29; Deut 34:8; Zech 9:11. There is a pious Catholic practice called the Heroic Act whereby a person pledges to God to offer all of his prayers and sacrifices during his life, as well as those suffrages that are offered for him after death, for the benefit of the Holy Souls.
261. In the book of Maccabees, we also see the high priest Onias and the prophet Jeremiah—who had been dead for many years—communicating with Judas Maccabeus and praying for the Jews on earth.
262. Cf. Mt 17:1–3; Mk 9:4; Lk 9:30–31.
263. Cf. Mt 27:47, 49; Mk 15:35–36.
264. Cf. Mt 27:52–53.

into eternity as "incense" before God.[265] These scriptures demonstrate that prayers from the living on earth influence those who are living in the afterlife, but who are not yet in heaven.

Protestants often argue that prayer cannot make satisfaction for sin because it is not penal, but pleasurable. This is only partly true. Some forms of prayer are joyful (prayers of adoration, thanksgiving), but other forms are works of satisfaction (prayers of repentance and forgiveness). When in the Our Father we pray to God to "forgive us our debts as we forgive our debtors," we are asking Him to forgive our sins and to free us from the debt of punishment. We see this with David's prayer of repentance: "Have mercy on me, O God, according to thy steadfast love . . . wash me thoroughly from my iniquity, and cleans me from my sin!" (Ps 51:1–2). When in prayer we pour out our sorrow for sin, the prayer becomes a penal work that makes satisfaction for sin.

Although the Holy Souls are members of the Mystical Body who are assisted by our prayers, we don't know for certain whether they're able to pray for us. Aquinas explained that we do not generally pray to the souls in purgatory for two reasons. First, although they are closer to God than we are, their suffering is greater than ours. This great suffering means that they are in no condition to pray for us but in a condition that demands our prayers for them. Secondly, because the Holy Souls do not yet enjoy the Beatific Vision, they're unable to know whether we're asking for their prayers. It appears that Thomas based his position on the premise that the souls cannot merit, and, hence, cannot hear our prayers. As always, Aquinas presents a reasonable case for his position.

---

265. Rev 5:8; 8:4; see also Rev 6:9–11.

Nevertheless, because the souls in purgatory are united to us by supernatural charity, there is no reason to contend that they are unable to pray for us. And of course, God could reveal to the Holy Souls our needs and requests. Nothing in Scripture or Tradition precludes such a possibility. Moreover, when the Book of Revelation refers to the "prayers of the saints,"[266] it does not say that these prayers come exclusively from those on earth. They could be coming from those in purgatory.

The word for "saint" (Hebrew, *qaddiysh*; Greek, *hagios*) simply means "holy one," and the Scriptures refer to living and deceased humans as saints.[267] If Scripture teaches that the saints in heaven respond to the prayers of those on earth (which it clearly does),[268] then it may be possible for the souls in purgatory to also respond to our prayers. This is why prominent theologians like Suarez and Bellarmine said that it was not only possible, but permissible, to appeal to the Holy Souls for their intercession.

2. Fasting

Fasting is the penitential act of abstaining from food or drink, either partially (for example, not eating meat or eating one meal a day) or completely (for example, consuming nothing, or water only). It is a penal work because it takes away from the sinner something that he desires. Because fasting tames the body's desire for food, it also subdues the lusts of the flesh. This is because the sensitive appetite is

---

266. Rev 5:8; 8:4.
267. Scripture refers to the deceased as "saints" in Mt 27:52; Eph 2:19; 3:18; Col 1:12; 2 Thess 1:10; Rev 5:8; 8:3–4; 11:18; 13:10.
268. Cf. Rev 6:9–11, where the saints in heaven respond to the imprecatory prayers of those on earth.

satisfied by carnal pleasure, namely food and sex. Hence, Paul says we must show ourselves as servants of God "in fastings and chastity."[269] Fasting promotes chastity just as gluttony promotes lust. If we cannot tame our natural passions, we will never prevail in the spiritual battle.

Fasting also raises the mind to the spiritual realm and makes us more docile to the will of God. This is why, after Daniel fasted for three weeks, he received a vision from God.[270] We also see how the apostles' fasts moved the Holy Spirit to guide them in ordaining new priests.[271] The preacher says, "I thought in my heart, to withdraw my flesh from wine, that I might turn my mind to wisdom, and might avoid folly."[272] Fasting bridles concupiscence by subjecting the flesh to the spirit, and this subjection leads the mind and heart to the things of heaven. Jesus also teaches us that fasting has tremendous power over the devil, such as in the case of the demon that could only be expelled from the possessed boy through "prayer and fasting." (Mk 9:29).

Finally, fasting makes satisfaction for sins because God responds by relenting of His punishments. Scripture provides us with many examples of how God accepts our fasts for this purpose. Scripture says God "repents of evil" when we come to him "with fasting, with weeping, and with mourning." (Joel 2:12–13). We see this in the book of Jonah, when both the people and the livestock of Nineveh abstained from all food and water, and then God "repented of the evil which he had said he would do to them." (3:7–10). We also see this in the book of Judith, when "the people fasted many days throughout Judea" and "the Lord heard their prayers

---

269. 2 Cor 6:5, 6 (DR).
270. Cf. Dan 10:1–21.
271. Cf. Acts 13:2–3; 14:23.
272. Eccl 2:3 (DR).

and looked upon their affliction." (4:13). Scripture provides many other like examples.²⁷³

While acknowledging these Old Testament practices, some Protestants deny that fasting is required in the New Testament. They point to Jesus' statement, "Can the wedding guests fast while the bridegroom is with them?"²⁷⁴ Of course, Jesus follows this statement by adding, "Then days will come, when the bridegroom is taken away from them, and then they will fast."²⁷⁵ Since Jesus has been "taken away" into heaven, we are living in the days when we "will fast." In fact, in Matthew 6:16–18 Jesus instructs us how to fast:

> And when you fast, do not look dismal, like the hypocrites, for they disfigure their faces that their fasting may be seen by men. Truly, I say to you, they have their reward. But when you fast, anoint your head and wash your face, that your fasting may not be seen by men but by your Father who is in secret; and your Father who sees in secret will reward you.

Finally, Catholics fast because Christ fasted, and we are called to be like Christ.²⁷⁶

Since apostolic times, the Church has required Catholics to abstain from flesh meat on Fridays, the day of Christ's

---

273. 2 Sam 23:16; Ez 8:21–23; 9:5; Neh 1:4; 9:1; Tob 12:8; Esth 4:3, 16; Ps 35:13; 69:10; 109:24; Jer 36:9; Dan 6:18; 9:3; Joel 1:14; 1 Macc 3:47; 2 Macc 13:12.
274. Mk 2:20; see also Mt 9:15; Lk 5:35.
275. Mt 9:15; see also Mk 2:20; Lk 5:35.
276. Cf. Mt 4:2; Lk 4:2. Curiously, some fundamentalists nonetheless condemn fasting, based on Paul's injunctions in 1 Tim 4:1–3. However, Paul was condemning those heretics who believed matter was evil, which is why Paul says in the next verse that "everything created by God is good, and nothing is to be rejected if it is received with thanksgiving." Moreover, Jesus exhorts us to fast to atone for sin and even gives us instructions on how to fast (Mt 6:16–18; see also 9:15; Mk 2:20; Lk 5:35).

Passion, to make satisfaction for their sins. In fact, throughout most of the Church's history, Catholics were required to abstain not only from meat (including meat gravy and soup), but also eggs and milk foods.[277] The Church imposed these requirements because meat and dairy products, being rich in substance, provide the most pleasure to the palate and also an incentive to lust (the main vice that fasting aims to conquer). Because the animals that walk the earth and breathe the air are more like man in body, they afford greater enjoyment and nourishment than other types of foods.

In the Church's traditional calendar, the days of complete abstinence are all Fridays, Ash Wednesday, Holy Saturday, and the Vigils of the Immaculate Conception and Christmas.[278] The days of partial abstinence are Ember Wednesdays and Saturdays (days at the beginning of certain seasons like Advent and Lent) and the Vigil of Pentecost. On days of complete abstinence, flesh meat, soup and gravy made from meat are not permitted at all. On days of partial abstinence, flesh meat, soup and gravy are permitted once a day at the principal meal.

All persons over seven years of age are bound to the law of abstinence. All persons over twenty-one and under sixty are bound to the law of fast. This means that on fast days they may have only one principal meal and two smaller, meatless meals (also called "collations") sufficient to maintain strength according to each one's needs. The two smaller

---

277. The Church no longer requires abstinence from dairy products during the prescribed days of fasting. However, the Church still requires abstinence from meat on all Fridays throughout the year, in accordance with the prescripts of the Conference of Catholic bishops. See canon law 1251. Also, canon 1253 allows the conference of bishops to permit the substitution of other forms of penance for abstinence and fast.

278. The Church allowed Catholics to anticipate this fast on December 23 (Sacred Congregation of the Council, December 3, 1959).

meals together should not equal one full meal. Eating between meals on fast days is not permitted, but liquids like milk and fruit juices may be taken any time. The Church has always granted dispensations from these requirements for serious reasons concerning health or the ability to work.

3. Almsgiving

Almsgiving, which literally means "mercy,"[279] is any material favor performed to assist the needy. Almsgiving must always be prompted by the virtue of charity, and not for selfish motives, for Paul makes the astonishing statement: "And if I should distribute all my goods to feed the poor, and if I should deliver my body to be burned, and have not charity, it profiteth me nothing."[280] Yet, while almsgiving is a work of mercy, it is also an act of justice that makes satisfaction for sin. This is because giving alms takes away from one who has and gives to one who has not. Because this act restores the equity of justice, it avails for the satisfaction of temporal punishments.

For example, Scripture says, "Blessed is he who considers the poor! The Lord delivers him in the day of trouble," wherein "the day" refers to one's purgatorial judgment by fire. (Ps 41:1). Sirach connects alms with purgatory when he says "Water quencheth a flaming fire, and alms resisteth sins."[281] Scripture further says, "For alms deliver from all sin, and from death, and will not suffer the soul to go into darkness."[282] Daniel says to king Nebuchadnezzar, "redeem thou

---

279. From the Greek *eleemosyne*.
280. 1 Cor 13:3 (DR). Paul's statement underscores that God accepts our penances only under the auspices of grace.
281. 3:33 (DR); see also Sir 4:1; 7:10; 12:3; 17:18; 29:15; 31:11 (DR).
282. Tob 4:11; see also Tob 4:12; 12:8–9.

thy sins with alms, and thy iniquities with works of mercy to the poor."[283] The Book of Proverbs succinctly summarizes the teaching: "charity covereth all sins."[284]

In the New Testament, Paul says, "Do not neglect to do good and to share what you have, for such sacrifices are pleasing to God," where "sacrifices" are acts that satisfy divine justice. (Heb 13:16). Jesus also says, "But yet that which remaineth, give alms; and behold, all things are clean unto you."[285] This is why the early Christians held everything in common and "sold their possessions and goods and distributed them to all, as any had need." (Acts 2:45). If we do not give our "pennies" away in this life, Jesus warns us that we will pay them in purgatory, even unto the very last one. (Mt 5:26). In short, Scripture clearly connects the giving of alms with making satisfaction for sins.

Not only does almsgiving atone for sin, but it is necessary for our salvation. If we fail to build with the "precious stones" of almsgiving and build only with "wood, hay, and stubble," God will destroy us at the Judgment. (1 Cor 3:17). Jesus is clear that our almsgiving—how we assist the hungry, the thirsty, the naked, the stranger—determines our eternal destiny. (Mt 25:31–46). For whatever we do to the least of our brothers, we do to Jesus Himself. That's why Jesus says, "Give to him who begs from you, and do not refuse him who would borrow from you." (Mt 5:42). James teaches that if a man neglects to give alms to the poor, his faith cannot save him. (Cf. 2:14–15). Such faith by itself, if it has no works, is dead (v. 17). John also asks, "But if any one has the world's goods and sees his brother in need, yet closes his heart against him, how does God's love abide in him?"

283. Dan 4:24 (DR).
284. 10:12 (DR).
285. Lk 11:41 (DR).

(I Jn 3:17). Such a man, John says, does not have "eternal life abiding in him" (v. 15).

Almsgiving includes giving not only to the poor but also to the Church. In the Old Testament, the faithful were required to give ten percent of their earnings to the house of God and to God's priests.[286] This portion was called a tithe, from the word *teotha*, meaning "a tenth." For example, Abraham gave the priest Melchizedek "a tenth of everything" after Melchizedek offered the bread-and-wine sacrifice to God.[287] Scripture instructs us to "dedicate your tithe with gladness. Give to the Most High as he has given, and as generously as your hand has found." (Sir 35:10).

The obligation to tithe to the priests of God continues in the New Covenant. Jesus teaches that "the laborer deserves his food."[288] Jesus was clear that "those who proclaim the gospel should get their living by the gospel." (I Cor 9:14). Thus, Paul repeats Jesus' teaching by saying, "You shall not muzzle an ox when it is treading out the grain," and, "The laborer deserves his wages."[289] Paul also says, "If we have sown spiritual good among you, is it too much if we reap your material benefits?" (I Cor 9:11). All the members of the Church have an obligation to support the ministers of the Church to further the proclamation of the gospel.

In fact, in the New Covenant, we have a *greater* obligation to tithe than our forefathers had in the Old Covenant. Jesus teaches us that "unless your righteousness exceeds that of the scribes and Pharisees, you will never enter the kingdom of heaven." (Mt 5:20). The Pharisees would give out of

---

286. Gen 28:22; Lev 27:30–32; Num 18:21, 24, 26, 28; Deut 12:6, 11, 17; 14:22–24, 28; 26:12, 14; Neh 12:44; 13:5, 12; Amos 4:4; Mal 3:8, 10; Tob 1:6; 5:13; Jdt 11:13; Sir 35:9; I Macc 3:49; 10:31; 11:35.
287. Cf. Gen 14:18–20.
288. Mt 10:10; Lk 10:7.
289. I Tim 5:18. See also I Cor 9:9; Deut 25:4.

their abundance, but we, like the poor widow, are required to give in abundance.[290] Jesus wants us to give until it hurts, because penal works are necessary to make satisfaction for sin. Avoiding purgatory means reaching perfection in this life, and we can do so through generous almsgiving. As Jesus said to the rich young man, "If you would be perfect, go, sell what you possess and give to the poor, and you will have treasure in heaven; and come, follow me." (Mt 19:21).

Although material almsgiving is an essential duty before God, spiritual almsgiving has even greater value; as Scripture says, "I will give you a good gift, forsake not my law."[291] Just as the soul is more excellent than the body, spiritual gifts are more excellent than corporeal gifts. Corporeal gifts benefit a person's temporal sustenance, whereas spiritual almsgiving benefits one's eternal sustenance. The work of apologetics and evangelization is one type of spiritual almsgiving. When our witness helps bring someone to the Catholic and apostolic faith, we make satisfaction for our sins. James says, "My brethren, if any one among you wanders from the truth and some one brings him back, let him know that whoever brings back a sinner from the error of his way will save his soul from death and will cover a multitude of sins." (5:19–20).

---

290. Cf. Lk 21:1–4. Jesus points out that, even though the Pharisees would "tithe mint and rue and every herb," they neglected justice and the love of God (Lk 11:42). Jesus' teaching emphasizes that we must give alms with true charity from God's grace, and not out of legal obligation.

291. Prov 4:2. The "spiritual works of mercy" are as follows: To instruct the ignorant; to counsel the doubtful; to admonish sinners; to bear wrongs patiently; to forgive offenses willingly; to comfort the afflicted; and to pray for the living and the dead. The "corporal works of mercy" are as follows: To feed the hungry; to give drink to the thirsty; to clothe the naked; to shelter the homeless; to visit the sick; to ransom the captive; and, to bury the dead.

The Sacraments

We now turn to a brief discussion on the sacraments. A sacrament is an outward sign instituted by Jesus Christ to give grace to the soul. Just as Jesus redeemed us through the sacrifice of His physical body, He applies the fruits of His redemptive work through His Mystical Body, the Catholic Church. This is why Paul says, "Christ loved the church and gave himself up for her, that he might sanctify her." (Eph 5:25–26). Christ "sanctifies" the Church—that is, the members of His body—through the sacraments. The sacraments derive their efficacy solely from the Passion of Jesus Christ. Jesus instituted seven sacraments of the New Law to be administered by His Church: Baptism, Penance (Confession), the Eucharist, Confirmation, Holy Matrimony, Holy Orders and Anointing of the Sick (Extreme Unction).[292]

We have already mentioned the salutary effects of the sacraments of baptism and confession.[293] In baptism, Christ cleanses the soul of all sin (both Original and actual) and remits all punishment (eternal and temporal) due to sin. As Ezekiel prophesied, "I will sprinkle clean water upon you, and you shall be clean from all your uncleannesses." (36:25).

---

292. When a priest confers a sacrament, it is said to be effected *ex opere operato* (Latin, "from the work having been performed"). This means that God confers His grace through the sacrament by the very fact that the act was performed (the validity of the sacrament does not depend on the priest's personal holiness). However, the effect upon the one receiving the sacrament works *ex opere operantis* (Latin, "from the work of the worker"). This means that he who receives the sacrament determines the work's efficacy, according to his disposition to receive grace.

293. Because a newborn baby does nothing of his own will to contract Original Sin, he doesn't need to do anything to receive the sacrament of baptism which washes away Original Sin. His sin is contracted by an extrinsic cause, and so it can be removed by an extrinsic cause. Because, with actual sin, a sinner engages his will, God requires the sinner to engage that same will to confess the sin in the Sacrament of Penance, which washes away the sin.

Paul explains that Christ sanctifies the Church by "having cleansed her by the washing of water with the word, that he might present the church to himself in splendor, without spot or wrinkle or any such thing, that she might be holy and without blemish." (Eph 5:26–27).

Because the "washing of water" (baptism) removes all sin and punishment from the soul, the soul is presented to Christ without stain or blemish. This is why Paul says, "you were washed, you were sanctified, you were justified in the name of the Lord Jesus Christ," where "sanctified" is in the Greek aorist past tense (*hagiazo*). Paul also says that because we have died with Christ in baptism, we also shall live with Christ.[294] This means that every baptized person is incorporated into the Passion of Jesus Christ as if he had suffered and died to make sufficient satisfaction for his sins (just like Christ made sufficient satisfaction for our sins). Because baptism is a rebirth in Christ that remits all sin and punishment, a soul can receive it only once. Let us now look in more detail at the sacrament of confession.

Confession: "If you forgive the sins of any, they are forgiven"

At the beginning of the second chapter, we saw various Scripture verses alluding to the Sacrament of Penance, also called confession or reconciliation. The Apostle John reveals that we must "confess our sins" in order for Christ to "forgive our sins and cleanse us" from evil. (1 Jn 1:9). When we confess our sins in the sacrament, Christ's atonement washes away our sins and then "there is no longer any

---

294. Cf. Rom 6:4–11.

offering for sin." (Heb 10:18). If, however, we fall back into sin, we must confess these new sins in the sacrament. If we do not confess our sins, "there no longer remains a sacrifice for sins," that is, Christ's atoning sacrifice will not be applied to us. (Heb 10:26).

We also saw how Jesus gave His apostles the authority to forgive sins when He told them: "If you forgive the sins of any, they are forgiven; if you retain the sins of any, they are retained." (Jn 20:23). Christ entrusted His Church with the authority to forgive sins when He promised to give Peter the keys: "I will give you the keys of the kingdom of heaven, and whatever you bind on earth shall be bound in heaven, and whatever you loose on earth shall be loosed in heaven." (Mt 16:19). Notice the parallels in these two verses. What is "forgiven" in John is considered "loosed" in Matthew, and what is "retained" in John is considered "bound" in Matthew. This means that the power to forgive/loose sin and retain/bind sin flows from the authority of the keys.

So what are the keys? The keys metaphorically represent Christ's authority over life and death.[295] Jesus says, "I died, and behold I am alive for evermore, and I have the keys of Death and Hades." (Rev 1:18). Because sin leads to death and forgiveness of sin leads to life, the keys symbolize the authority to forgive and retain sin. Because the stain of sin and the debt of punishment prevent one from entering the kingdom of heaven, the "keys to the kingdom of heaven" open the door by forgiving sin and remitting punishment, and shut the door to the kingdom by retaining sin and imposing punishment.

The Book of Revelation reveals, "The words of the holy one, the true one, who has the key of David, who opens and

---

295. For an in-depth analysis of the meaning of the keys, please see my book *The Biblical Basis for the Papacy* (Our Sunday Visitor).

no one shall shut, who shuts and no one opens." (3:7). Just as the prime minister to the king of the old Davidic kingdom had the "key" to "open and shut,"[296] the prime minister (the pope) to the King (Jesus) of the new Davidic kingdom (the Catholic Church) has the key to bind and loose. Only now, the keys of the kingdom, which Jesus gives to Peter, open the door not to a temporal kingdom, but to the eternal kingdom of heaven itself. This is why Jesus says that what is bound or loosed on earth is ratified in heaven. This is also why the sacrament of confession is necessary for salvation for all who commit actual sin.

While Christ delegated His keys to Peter alone (and to his successors through the passing of the keys), the other apostles who were united to Christ through Peter also shared in his binding and loosing authority. (Cf. Mt 18:18). The apostles handed on their authority to successors, and they to their successors, and so on all the way down to the present age. Thus, all the bishops of the Catholic Church, who trace their priestly ordinations back to the original apostles, share in the power of the keys. This means that Catholic bishops and the priests they ordain have the authority to forgive sins. This is why Paul describes the priests of the Church "as servants of Christ and stewards of the mysteries of God." (1 Cor 4:1).

Through the Sacrament of Penance, the priest, through the power of the keys, forgives the sinner both his mortal and venial sins. As in baptism, the grace that God infuses into the soul in the sacrament of confession remits the guilt and the eternal debt of punishment (hell) due to sin. However, unlike baptism, which remits all debt (eternal and temporal) of punishment, confession does not remit the entire debt of temporal punishment (although it lessens the debt, through

---

296. Cf. Isa 22:22.

the Church's authority to "loose").²⁹⁷ This is because, in baptism, man receives a new life in Christ, and nothing of his former life (including all sin and punishment) remains. In confession, the man is not born again, but healed.

Thus, just as the sinner was responsible for committing the sins that he confessed in the sacrament, God requires the sinner to take responsibility in making satisfaction for those sins—either in this life, or in the next. Although the Sacrament of Penance remits only the punishment of the one confessing the sins (and not the punishment of those in purgatory), we will see at the end of this chapter how the power of the keys can remit the punishments of the Holy Souls as well (through "indulgences").

What happens to a man who falls back into sin after confession? Some contend that his forgiven sins and related punishments return after he commits the same sins, because Ezekiel says, "But when a righteous man turns away from his righteousness and commits iniquity . . . [n]one of the righteous deeds which he has done shall be remembered." (Ezek 18:24). Yet in this verse, God does not mean that prior sins or punishments return, but only that a man's former good deeds are no benefit to him when he is in mortal sin. For Scripture says that God's "work is perfect." (Deut 32:4) and thus His work of forgiveness is perfect. God does not repent of his work of forgiveness. (Cf. Rom 11:29). This means that a man's subsequent sin cannot undo the prior forgiveness that God gave him. This also means that God forgives *all* the sins of a repentant sinner, not just some of his sins, just as God

---

297. The debt of temporal punishment is remitted according to the disposition of the penitent. The more frequently he approaches the sacrament, the more he is disposed to receive grace. As his grace increases, the stains of his sin decrease, which means the punishment required to remove the stains also decreases. A person's disposition to grace may be so great that, through frequent confession, his entire debt of punishment may be remitted.

demands satisfaction for all sins, down to the "last penny."

Many Catholics wonder whether, after their sins are for-given in confession, they return to the state of grace and vir-tue they had before committing mortal sin. It is clear that a man receives the gratuitous virtues in confession because he is infused in this sacrament with the grace from which these virtues flow. However, because he owes satisfaction for his sins, he is not in the same position as he was before.

Nevertheless, a man may be restored to a lesser, equal, or even greater grace than he had before, depending upon how his free will is disposed to receive God's grace. If for example he has a firmer purpose of amendment and greater desire for grace, he may arise to a greater level of grace, even though his debt of punishment has increased. In the story of the prodigal son, this restoration is symbolized by the father clothing his repentant son with "the best robe." (Lk 15:22). This is why God says to the repentant sinner, "I will restore to you the years which the swarming locust has eaten . . . You shall eat in plenty and be satisfied." (Joel 2:25–26).

Before closing this section, let us recall that Jesus gave the apostles the power not only to loose but to bind. "Loosing," of course, refers to forgiving sins. But what does "binding" refer to? Binding refers to imposing punishments for sin. Just as God both spares and inflicts punishments for sin, His priests also are able both to remit and impose punish-ments for sin. A priest can bind a sinner to punishment in two ways. First, by withholding forgiveness from a sinner (that is, not "loosing" the sin) who demonstrates a lack of contrition for his sins.[298] Secondly, by imposing a penance

---

298. This may happen when a penitent declares to the priest in the confessional that he will not terminate his sinful lifestyle (e.g., living in adultery, main-taining a pro-abortion position, keeping a membership in Freemasonry, etc.).

upon a sinner as condition for making satisfaction for his forgiven sins.

The Mass:
"Do this in remembrance of Me"

We have seen how the Church Fathers frequently refer to the Sacrifice of the Mass as assisting the souls in purgatory. We see these references as early as A.D. 211 in the writings of Tertullian, as well as among great Fathers like Cyril of Jerusalem, Ambrose and Augustine. Many saints[299] have received very vivid revelations of souls leaving the flames of purgatory by virtue of the Mass. Imploring forgiveness for the sins of the dead at the Mass has been the practice of the Catholic Church since the very beginning. Every November 2 the Church specifically offers its Masses throughout the world for the souls in purgatory (in fact, the Church devotes the entire month of November to assisting the Holy Souls). The Mass assists the Holy Souls because it is a sacrifice and, therefore, has satisfactory power.[300] This means we can and should offer the Mass with the intention of remitting punishment for sin, both for the living and the dead.

As we have demonstrated throughout this book, we, as members of the Body of Christ, can make satisfaction for another's sins. This means that we can intentionally offer the sacrifice of the Mass for the benefit of another, either living or dead, and God is sure to apply its benefits to that

---

299. E.g., Elizabeth, Nicholas, Henry Suso, John of Alvernia, Malachy, and Magdalen de Pazzi.

300. The Council of Trent even condemned those who said that the Mass "ought not to be offered for the living and the dead, for sins, punishments, satisfactions, and other necessities." Canon 3, Canons on the Sacrifice of the Mass, Session XXII (September 17, 1562).

person, according to his disposition. This can be done formally (by making arrangements with the priest to offer the Mass for that intention) or informally (by intention only). Whereas only those with the keys (the ministerial priests of the Church) have the power to offer the Mass, all of the baptized (the royal priests) are able to benefit from the Holy Sacrifice. Although an explanation of the scriptural basis for the Mass is beyond the scope of this section, let us look at some biblical background to the Church's theology of the Mass and how it assists the souls in purgatory.[301]

We must first mention that Catholics do not view the Mass as a new sacrifice, or think that it adds anything to the sacrifice of Christ. This would be impossible, for Christ's single sacrifice "is the expiation for our sins, and not for ours only but also for the sins of the whole world." (1 Jn 2:2). Rather, the Mass re-presents the same sacrifice that Christ offered on Calvary in a sacramental and unbloody manner, because Christ's infinite sacrifice transcends time and space. In describing the Mass, Paul says, "For Christ our pasch is sacrificed. Therefore let us feast."[302]

When the priest repeats the words of consecration that Jesus used at the Last Supper, God makes Christ's single and eternal sacrifice present upon Catholic altars. In this way, God applies the merits of Christ's infinite sacrifice to sinners of all times and places. This is why, after Jesus revealed to the apostles, "this is my body" and "this is my blood," He commanded them: "Do this in remembrance of me."[303] The Greek word for "remembrance" is *anamnesis* which refers

---

301. For a detailed, Scriptural explanation of the Holy Mass, please see my book *The Biblical Basis for the Eucharist* (Our Sunday Visitor).
302. 1 Cor 5:7–8 (DR).
303. Cf. Mt 26:26–28; Mk 14:22–24; Lk 22:19–20; 1 Cor 11:23–25.

to a "memorial sacrifice."[304] This means that Jesus' literally commanded His apostles, "Offer this as my memorial
sacrifice."

In establishing the Eucharistic sacrifice, Jesus fulfilled the
prophecies of the prophet Malachi. Malachi revealed that
God would someday reject the sacrifices of the Old Law and
institute a new offering: "For from the rising of the sun to its
setting my name is great among the nations, and in every place
incense is offered to my name, and a pure offering; for my
name is great among the nations, says the LORD of hosts."[305]
With this prophecy, Malachi reveals that God would estab-
lish single sacrifice that would be offered around the clock,
in every place—including among the Gentiles. Malachi later
confirms that this is the sacrifice of the new "covenant," when
the "Lord will suddenly come to his temple." (3:1).

Interestingly, Malachi makes a connection between the
New Covenant sacrifice and God's purification of the sons
of the Church: "For he is like a refiner's fire and like fuller's
soap; he will sit as a refiner and purifier of silver, and he will
purify the sons of Levi and refine them like gold and silver, till they present right offerings to the Lord." (3:2–3).
This is the Eucharistic sacrifice that Paul says shall "purify
your conscience from dead works to serve the living God."
(Heb 9:14). The early Church Fathers were unanimous in
their interpretation that Malachi's prophecy referred to the
Sacrifice of the Mass, which purifies both the living and the

---

304. In Hebrew, this Greek term comes from *zikaron* (*zakar*). In the context of
the Passover meal, the term referred to making the event (the Passover)
"truly present," not simply calling the event to mind. The only other time
anamnesis is used in the New Testament is in Hebrews 10:3 where Paul is
referring to the Levitical sacrifices under the Old Law.

305. Mal 1:11. Malachi uses the Hebrew *minchah* which is a singular noun to
describe the sacrifice that will be offered "in every place" and "from the
rising of the sun to its setting."

dead. No Christian disputed this revealed truth until the Protestant rebellion in the sixteenth century.

In the same Epistle to the Hebrews, Paul alludes to Malachi's prophecy when he describes the heavenly priesthood of Christ. After Paul explains that God in both the Old and New Covenants required the shedding of blood to forgive sins,[306] Paul describes the respective rites by saying, "Thus it was necessary for the copies of the heavenly things to be purified with these rites [Old Covenant], but the heavenly things themselves with better sacrifices [New Covenant] than these." (Heb 9:23). As we can plainly see, even though Christ offered His Calvary sacrifice once-for-all, Paul refers to the New Covenant sacrifice as "sacrifices," in the plural. Paul's use of the plural makes sense only if he is describing Christ's sacrifice in the context of its sacramental re-presentation "in every place" around the world in the Holy Mass.

Further, Paul reveals that the "heavenly things" are "purified" by these "better sacrifices." The "heavenly things" refer to the people of the New Covenant, just as the "copies of the heavenly things" referred to the "people" of the Old Covenant (cf. v. 19). Once again, this means that those in the New Covenant are purified from their sin and punishment through the sacrifice of the Mass. This purification from sin, which is the object of liturgical sacrifice, applies not only to those on earth, but also to those in purgatory. As royal priests in the one priesthood of Jesus Christ, we can make satisfaction for sin and punishment throughout the Mystical Body by uniting our "spiritual sacrifices" to our Lord's sacrifice. (See 1 Pet 2:5). This is yet another way we can make up with our own sacrifices what is lacking in the sufferings of Christ, for the sake of the Church. (Cf. Col 1:24).

---

306. Cf. Heb 9:18–22.

How is the New Covenant sacrifice offered? It is offered in the same manner as Melchizedek's sacrifice. As we saw earlier, Melchizedek is the first priest mentioned in the Old Testament who offered a sacrifice of bread and wine. (Gen 14:18). Paul reveals that Jesus' priesthood in heaven is modeled after that of Melchizedek.[307] Note, however, that when Paul makes the bread and wine connection between Jesus and Melchizedek, he never mentions the Last Supper. Instead, Paul is referring to Christ's heavenly priesthood, which He exercises through His New Covenant priests on earth (those men who are offering "better sacrifices" than those of the Old Covenant). Thus, Christ is a priest in the same manner as Melchizedek because He makes His priestly sacrifice present through His ministerial priests under the appearance of bread and wine in the Holy Mass.

Following the sacrifice of the Mass, wherein the priest changes bread and wine into the body and blood of Christ, Catholics receive the Sacrament of the Eucharist, also called Holy Communion. Jesus says, "Truly, truly, I say to you, unless you eat the flesh of the Son of man and drink his blood, you have no life in you; he who eats my flesh and drinks my blood has eternal life, and I will raise him up at the last day. For my flesh is food indeed and my blood is drink indeed. He who eats my flesh and drinks my blood abides in me, and I in him." (Jn 6:53–56). By consuming Christ's flesh and blood, Catholics receive an infusion of grace that washes away venial sin, remits the debt of temporal punishment, and increases their merits for greater glory in heaven.[308] Catholics can offer the satisfactory benefits

---

307. Cf. Heb 5:6, 10; 6:20; 7:15, 17; see also Ps 110:4.
308. Because Jesus says, "if any one eats of this bread, he will live forever" (Jn 6:51) and "living forever" is the life of glory, partaking of the Eucharist on earth is the pledge of future glory in heaven.

from Communion for their souls as well as for the souls in purgatory.

What about those in mortal sin? Are they forgiven of their sin through the sacrament of the Eucharist? No, they are not. Although it's true that an infusion of grace can wash away mortal sin, this forgiveness must come from the Sacrament of Penance. Because a person turns away from God by committing mortal sin through an act of pride, God requires the sinner to return to Him through an act of humility: confessing his sins to a priest. This humbling and penitential act is a movement contrary to the sinner's proud and stubborn will and begins in earnest the process of making satisfaction for his sins.

In fact, if a person receives the Eucharist while in a state of mortal sin, he commits another mortal sin by doing so and compounds the gravity of his spiritual condition. Paul says, "Whoever, therefore, eats the bread or drinks the cup of the Lord in an unworthy manner will be guilty of profaning the body and blood of the Lord. For any one who eats and drinks without discerning the body eats and drinks judgment upon himself."[309] The Greek word for "judgment" (*krima*) that Paul uses refers to nothing less than eternal damnation.[310] Why would Paul impose the harshest of all penalties for receiving the Eucharist in a state of mortal sin? Because receiving the Eucharist is an actual "participation in the body and blood of Christ."[311] When we receive the Eucharist, we

---

309. 1 Cor 11:27, 29.
310. See, for example, Rom 2:2–3; 3:6, 8; 5:16; 1 Tim 3:6; 5:12; Heb 6:2 where Paul uses the same word to describe eternal condemnation. Paul's penalty for receiving the Eucharist unworthily demonstrates that the Eucharist is not just a symbol (but instead the actual body of Christ) because one cannot be liable to eternal hell-fire for abusing a symbol.
311. Cf. 1 Cor 10:16–17. The Greek word for "participation" (*koinonia*) refers to an actual, intimate communion with the thing in question.

"become partakers of the divine nature." (2 Pet 1:4). We commune with Jesus Christ Himself. Because Christ is "the light of the world"[312] and a person in mortal sin is in darkness (because he has no grace), the light and darkness cannot be mixed without committing sacrilege. Holiness cannot be a partaker with sin. As Paul says, "Or what fellowship has light with darkness? Therefore come out from them, and be separate from them, says the Lord, and touch nothing unclean." (2 Cor 6:14,17).

Extreme Unction:
"Is any man sick among you?"

Jesus Christ instituted the Sacrament of Extreme Unction (also called "Anointing of the Sick") to commend those who are seriously ill to the mercy of God, so that He might heal them both spiritually and physically. This is another sacrament that forgives sin and remits punishment to help souls avoid purgatory. A priest confers this sacrament upon those who are in danger of death by anointing the parts of their body with blessed oil. The parts of the body that are anointed are those parts that were used to commit sin—the eyes, ears, nose, tongue, hands and feet. Mark in his gospel refers to the apostles conferring this sacrament when he records, "And they cast out many demons, and anointed with oil many that were sick and healed them."[313]

The Scriptural basis for this sacrament is found quite explicitly in the Epistle of James: "Is any among you sick? Let him call for the elders [priests] of the church, and let

---

312. Jn 8:12; 9:5.
313. 6:13. Many of the Church Fathers wrote about the sacrament of Extreme Unction, including Ambrose, Cyril of Alexandria, Ephraem, Hippolytus, John Chrysostom, Origen, and Tertullian.

them pray over him, anointing him with oil in the name of the Lord; and the prayer of faith will save the sick man, and the Lord will raise him up; and if he has committed sins, he will be forgiven." (Jas 5:14–15). This is another passage in Scripture that proves the priests of Christ's Church have the authority to forgive sins. Although Protestant groups sometimes conduct "healing prayers" by calling upon the prayers of their pastors, nowhere in their theology or practice do they accommodate priestly forgiveness of sin, which is set forth so clearly in this passage by the Apostle James. Let's look briefly at some of the elements of this sacrament.

The sacrament is administered only to those who are in danger of death. Mark refers to those "that were sick" and James also asks, "Is any among you sick?" (which is why this sacrament is often called "the sacrament of the sick").[314] The sacrament is not administered to those in good health, however it is also not deferred until someone is at the very point of death. This is because one of the purposes of the sacrament is bodily healing (although this is of secondary importance).[315] Also, if a person's reasoning and consciousness are impaired through illness, his mind will be unable to direct his will to participate in the graces conferred, and this inability may diminish the sacrament's efficacy. We also

---

314. Just as the sacrament of baptism is signified by a physical washing with water, the sacrament of the sick is signified by a physical anointing with oil. Water is connected to washing and oil to healing, which signifies that baptism is a spiritual regeneration and Extreme Unction is a spiritual healing.

315. Because spiritual healing is the principal effect of this sacrament, physical healing (the secondary effect) may not necessarily follow, except when it is requisite for the spiritual healing. This is exemplified by the paralytic in Luke's gospel (chapter 5). The principal effect of Christ's healing was the forgiveness of his sins (v. 20), and the secondary effect was the physical healing of his malady (v. 24). Because the sacrament may bring about physical healing, it can be repeated.

note that the sacrament is often conferred upon those who are not sick but have a sure prospect of death, such as those who are going to war or who have been condemned to death by the state.

The principal benefit of this sacrament is the forgiveness of sin. As James says, "the prayer of faith will save the sick man" and "if he has committed sins, he will be forgiven." Because Christ instituted the sacraments of baptism and confession to wash away grave sin, Extreme Unction is primarily ordered to the forgiveness of lesser sin. Mortal sin can impede the grace of the sacrament, which is why priests desire to administer the sacrament of confession before anointing, if the person is capable of confessing his sins. Hence, Baptism and Confession are directed toward the obstacles that deprive a man of spiritual life (Original Sin and actual mortal sin), whereas Extreme Unction is directed toward the defects that weaken a man's spiritual life (venial sin and remnants of sin).

The Catechism of the Council of Trent states that the sacrament "liberates the soul from the languor and infirmity which it contracted from sins, and from all the other remains of sin."[316] Thus, the grace of the sacrament of anointing remits all venial sin (the "wood, hay, and stubble") as well as remnants of sin, that is, those lingering defects that otherwise prevent the soul's total and complete union with God—the defects that detain souls in purgatory. On these points, Aquinas says that the grace of the sacrament moves the free will to be sorrowful for sin, and this contrition removes the stain of sin as the sinner is so disposed. He also says that God does not lessen the measure of satisfaction required for sin, but that the debt of punishment is diminished because

---

316. *Catechism of the Council of Trent* (South Bend, IN: Marian Publications, 1976), pages 314–415.

the person is able, through the grace of the sacrament, to bear his punishment more easily.

Nevertheless, through the power of the keys and the treasury of the Church, the priest is able to remit all the sick person's temporal punishment so long as there is no obstacle preventing this great grace. The priest remits the temporal punishment of the sick person's sins through what is called the "Apostolic Blessing" conferred upon the sick person at the conclusion of the Sacrament of Extreme Unction. The priest says, "By the Faculty which the Apostolic See has given me, I grant you a plenary indulgence for the remission of all your sins, and I bless you. In the Name of the Father and the Son + and the Holy Sprit. Amen."[317] We shall see in the next section what is meant by a "plenary indulgence."

The sacrament also strengthens the sick person against the attacks of the devil. At no time does the devil work harder at trying to deprive us of hope in God than when we are facing the end of our lives. As the Book of Wisdom says, "They will come with dread when their sins are reckoned up, and their lawless deeds will convict them to their face." (4:20). Man dreads nothing more than to face his own death, at which time he recalls all of his past sins and anticipates God's pending judgment upon him. The sacrament of anointing infuses the soul with graces to help the soul fight bravely against the adversary and surrender itself to the mercy of God.

To assist in this battle, the priest will also give the sick person the flesh and blood of Jesus Christ in the Sacrament of the Eucharist. When it is given to the dying the Eucharist is called Viaticum, which is Latin for "food for the journey." All these graces, which flow from the Passion of Christ, prepare

---

317. The Apostolic Blessing is always given in the old Latin rite: "*Ego facultate mihi ab Apostolic Sede tributa, indulgentiam plenariam et remissionem omnium peccatorum tibi concedo et benedico te. In nomine Patris, et Fílii, et Spiritus Sancti. Amen.*"

the soul for immediate entrance into heaven, thereby avoiding the need for purgatory. As Scripture says, "Blessed are the dead who die in the Lord." (14:13).

Indulgences

"Whatever you loose on earth shall be loosed in heaven"

In addition to prayer, fasting, almsgiving, and the sacraments, obtaining indulgences is one of the most powerful means of assisting the souls in purgatory and expiating our own punishments while on earth.[318] Many of the Church Fathers wrote about indulgences, including Tertullian, Cyprian, Gregory of Nyssa, Basil, Cummian, and Bede. The Church defines an indulgence as a remission before God of the temporal punishment due to sins whose guilt has already been forgiven. The faithful Catholic who is duly disposed gains an indulgence under certain defined conditions through the Church's help when, as a minister of redemption, it dispenses and applies with authority the treasury of satisfactions won by Christ and the saints.[319]

As with the Church's authority to forgive sin, a person obtains an indulgence through the Church by virtue of the power of the keys.[320] This means that the authority of granting indulgences rests with the pope who alone holds the keys.[321] We recall that Christ promised to Peter that what-

318. We must remember that prayers and good works are much more valuable than indulgences because indulgences remit temporal punishment, while prayers and good works also mean an increase of grace and merit for all eternity.

319. Cf. Pope Paul VI, *Indulgentiarum Doctrina* (January 1, 1967), Nos. 7–8.

320. Mt 16:19; CCC 1478.

321. Although the pope alone holds the keys, bishops in union with the pope share in the power of the keys. This means that bishops and their delegates

ever he bound or loosed on earth would be bound or loosed in heaven. (Cf. Mt 16:19). By using the term "whatever" (Greek, *ho ean*), Christ empowered Peter with a broad and plenary power to remit not only sin but the punishments for sin as well. If Jesus granted His priests the authority to remove the eternal penalty of sin (through the sacrament of confession), it logically follows that priests have the authority to remit the temporal punishments due to sin as well.

The Church is able (through the power of the keys) to remit temporal punishment due to sin because of its treasury of merits. This treasury, as we have mentioned, includes not only the superabundant merits of Jesus Christ but also the abundant merits of the saints. By God's grace, many members of the Mystical Body have performed works of satisfaction that exceed the requirement of their debts. These works include not only voluntary penances but also the patient endurance of the scourges of this world, with the intention of making reparation for sin. In fact, the quantity of these merits is so great that it exceeds the entire debt of punishment due from the rest of the members of the Body of Christ.[322] These merits, along with the infinite merits of Christ, are the common property of the whole Church and are distributed to the members of the body according to the judgment of the Vicar of Christ who holds the keys to the kingdom of heaven.

While indulgences can be applied to both the living and the dead,[323] there is an important distinction in their

---

can also grant indulgences subject to the pope's ordination. Further, even one who is in mortal sin can grant indulgences, because mortal sin doesn't cause a loss of jurisdiction and because he remits punishment by virtue of the merits in the Church's treasury and not his own merits (or demerits).

322. Cf. *Summa Theologica*, Supp. Q. 25, Art 1.
323. CCC 1471. The "living" means the one doing the indulgenced work. A person cannot apply an indulgence to another living person. Indulgences

application: those who are living on earth are subject to the Church's immediate jurisdiction whereas those who have died are subject directly to God's jurisdiction. Thus, the Church grants indulgences to the living as an exercise of its judicial authority, but applies indulgences to the dead by way of petition. That is, the Church implores God to apply the indulgence to the intended soul in purgatory by accepting the works of satisfaction that have been performed to that end. This means we cannot be certain that God will apply the indulgence to a particular soul, but we piously believe that the intended soul will benefit from the indulgence in some way.[324] That having been said, we know with certainty that God will apply the indulgence to a soul or souls according to His infinite standards of justice.

Unfortunately, there are many misconceptions about indulgences, even among Catholics. For example, some people think that a person can "buy his way out of hell" with an indulgence. This can't be true, first of all, because indulgences remit temporal punishment only—not the eternal punishment of hell. Furthermore, one must be in a state of grace to receive an indulgence. That is, the recipient of an indulgence must be united to the One who merited the indulgence.

Neither does an indulgence guarantee a person's salvation or allow him to "indulge" in sin. One who receives an indulgence can still fall into mortal sin and lose his soul. An

---

can only be applied to someone in accordance with the intention of the grantor, and since the Church applies the indulgence to the doer of the work, the doer cannot transfer the intention to another.

324. Aquinas teaches that indulgences principally profit the living person who avails himself of an indulgence because he does the work for which the indulgence is granted; and secondarily and indirectly profit the dead for whom one does what is the cause of the indulgence (since that person doesn't perform the indulgenced work, but only receives its benefits).

indulgence does not pardon future sin, but only it remits the punishment due to past sin already forgiven.

Before the Second Vatican Council, the Church would declare that a particular indulgence would equate to a certain number of days of penance. By reciting a certain prayer, a person might gain an indulgence of, for example, 100 days. This meant that the remission of temporal punishment associated with that particular indulgence would be proportionate to performing 100 days of penance. Using "days" in this fashion confused some people who erroneously thought that the "days" ascribed to a particular indulgence denoted the amount of "time off" from purgatory that the penitent would receive. To eliminate the confusion, Pope Paul VI revised the Church's practice in his *Enchiridion of Indulgences* (1968) which no longer attributes days to indulgenced works. Instead, indulgences are either plenary (all temporal punishment is removed) or partial (some temporal punishment is removed).

Like the dogma of purgatory, indulgences are part of the Church's infallible teaching (the popes have "bound" us to the teaching). The Council of Trent, which also defined the dogma of purgatory, declared:

> Since the power of granting indulgences has been given to the Church by Christ, and since the Church from the earliest times has made use of this Divinely given power, the holy synod teaches and ordains that the use of indulgences, as most salutary to Christians and as approved by the authority of the councils, shall be retained by the Church; and if further pronounces anathema against those who either declare that indulgences are useless

or deny that the Church has the power to grant them.[325]

Hence, it is necessary for all Catholics to believe in indulgences. To deny the Church's power to grant indulgences is to deny a revealed truth of the Catholic faith.

Didn't the Church Once Sell Indulgences?

Unfortunately, hundreds of years ago there were certain abuses in the Church's administration of indulgences, and it almost never fails that an anti-Catholic accuses the Church of having "sold indulgences" for pecuniary gain. Of course, whether there were abuses in granting indulgences has no bearing upon whether the doctrine of indulgences is true or false. There were also many abuses in the early apostolic Church, but that didn't mean that the apostles threw out the Deposit of Faith and started over (which is essentially what the Protestant "Reformers" did). For example, just because the Corinthians were abusing the Eucharist didn't mean that Paul told them to give up the Church's doctrines on the Eucharist. (Cf. 1 Cor 11:27–30).

Trumped-up charges of indulgence-selling are usually advanced by those who don't even know what indulgences are, and even if they did, would not accept the Church's authority to grant them.

It is true that, during certain periods in Church history, certain clergy of the Church did abuse the practice of administering indulgences. These abuses primarily concerned clerics asking for financial contributions from their parishioners.

---

325. Council of Trent, Session 25 (December 4, 1563). See also Pope Leo X, Exsurge Domine (June 15, 1520); the Council of Constance, Session 8 (May 4, 1415); and Pope Clement VI, Unigenitus (January 27, 1343).

Although some of these clerics were motivated by selfish reasons, many others were motivated to raise money for the poor of the parish and other praiseworthy objectives. There is nothing intrinsically evil about encouraging the faithful to give alms to the poor, to build a church, or to endow a hospital in thanksgiving for receiving an indulgence. It is only when a priest deliberately requires a temporal price in consideration for a spiritual favor, otherwise known as "simony," that condemnation is warranted.[326] But as a matter of official practice, the Catholic Church never sold indulgences. And even where abuses did occur, the faithful still received the great benefits of the indulgences, which nourished their spiritual lives and pleased God.[327]

While Protestants are quick to make a connection between the abuses involving indulgences and Luther's revolt in the sixteenth century, most of these varied and isolated abuses— and the Church's condemnation of them—came well before the Reformation. For example, the Fourth Lateran Council (1215) put limits on the use and benefits of indulgences granted for dedicating a church. Similar prescriptions were adopted at regional councils in Vienna (1311) and Ravenna (1317). Pope Boniface IX (1392) condemned certain clerics in the diocese of Ferrara who were exacting money in exchange for indulgences. Pope Martin V (1450) and Pope Sixtus IV (1478) also issued negative judgments concerning

326. The term *simony* is taken from the man Simon who offered the apostles money in the hope that they would give him the power of the Holy Spirit through the laying on of hands (Acts 8:18–19).

327. The most infamous case of purported abuse involved one Johann Tetzel, who was a preacher of indulgences under Pope Julius II. In 1517, Pope Julius granted a plenary indulgence to those who confessed their sins, received the Eucharist, and contributed according to their means toward the construction of St. Peter's Basilica in Rome. Luther accused Tetzel of selling these indulgences in Germany, which was a pretext for his doctrinal defection from the Church.

certain abuses of indulgences. In order to protect the great benefit of indulgences, the Council of Trent ordered all abuses to be abolished.[328] In 1567, Pope St. Pius V canceled all grants of indulgences involving any fees. Given the Church's efforts to correct them, Luther's tirade against these abuses—and his ultimate rejection of the Catholic faith—is a perfect example of "throwing the baby out with the bathwater."

Scriptural Support for Indulgences

Scripture clearly teaches that God lessens the temporal punishment for sin based on the actions of others (which is precisely what an indulgence is). For example, in the Old Testament, we read that King Solomon loved many pagan women. In fact, he had 700 wives and 300 concubines! These associations ultimately led him to worship the women's pagan deities. (Cf. 1 Kg 11:1–8). Because Solomon's idolatry was a grievous breach of God's covenant, God would punish Solomon. He tells the king, "Since this has been your mind and you have not kept my covenant and my statutes which I have commanded you, I will surely tear the kingdom from you and will give it to your servant." (1 Kg 11:11). The temporal punishment for Solomon's sin was the loss of his kingdom.

However, this punishment would not happen in Solomon's lifetime. God continues, "Yet for the sake of David your father I will not do it in your days, but I will tear it out of the hand of your son. However I will not tear away all the kingdom; but I will give one tribe to your son, for the sake of David my servant and for the sake of Jerusalem which I have

---

328. Council of Trent, Session 25 (December 3–4, 1563).

chosen."[329] Thus, "for the sake of David and Jerusalem," God lessens Solomon's temporal punishment by deferring the divestiture of his kingdom and keeping one tribe (Benjamin) under the dominion of Judah. In other words, God gives Solomon an indulgence. If it weren't for David's merits before God, God would have removed the entire kingdom from Solomon and during his reign.

God does a similar thing with another king of Israel named Ahab, in I Kings chapter 21. Ahab coveted a certain vineyard in Jezreel which was located near his palace. The vineyard was owned by a man named Namoth. Ahab tries to convince Namoth to sell or exchange it so that Ahab could take possession of it. But Namoth refuses, and Ahab in anger consents to Namoth's death. Like his predecessor Solomon, Ahab falls into the grave sin of idolatry. For these sins, God reveals through Elijah that He was going to destroy Ahab and his kingdom: "Behold, I will bring evil upon you; I will utterly sweep you away" (v. 21).

Upon hearing these words, Scripture says that Ahab "rent his clothes, and put sackcloth upon his flesh, and fasted and lay in sackcloth, and went about dejectedly" (v. 27). Ahab's severe penances make some satisfaction for his sins, and God responds by having mercy on him, saying, "Because he has humbled himself before me, I will not bring the evil in his days; but in his son's days I will bring the evil upon his house" (v. 29). As with Solomon, God gives Ahab an indulgence. Because of Ahab's penance, God lessens Ahab's temporal punishments by deferring them to his successor's reign.[330]

---

329. Vv. 12–13. See also Isa 37:35.
330. God does the same thing with Joram, the son of Ahab. Joram also did evil in the sight of the Lord, but the Lord diminished his temporal punishments "for the sake of David his servant" (2 Kg 8:19).

Similarly, during the Exodus when God wanted to kill all the Jews as a punishment for their idolatry, Moses begs God to relent of His punishment by offering Him a penance of fasting for forty days and nights.[331] On account of Moses' sacrifice, God lessens the Jews' punishment by merely sending them a plague—a partial indulgence that preserves many of their lives.

Paul emphasizes how God has tempered His punishments of the Jews in spite of their sinfulness, since "they are beloved for the sake of their forefathers." (Rom 11:28). As with Solomon, Ahab and many other Jews of the Old Testament, God would lessen their temporal punishments because of the faithfulness and penances of their ancestors.[332] This is why Paul says, "For the gifts and the calling of God are without repentance."[333] God does not regret calling the Jews to salvation, for His promise to save them through Jesus Christ is unchangeable.[334]

---

331. Deut 9:18–19; 25–29.

332. In Rom 9:4–5, Paul refers to the gifts with which God had blessed the Jews which surely played a part in His deferring their immediate punishment for rejecting Him (see Rom 9:27; 11:4–5, 14, 20–21, 25). Note also that there is no verb (e.g., "belong") in this passage ("*Israelites hos ho huiothesia kai ho doxa kai ho*"). Thus, it is incorrect to say that these gifts still belong to the Jews, which would undermine the Jews' call to salvation exclusively through the New Covenant of Jesus Christ.

333. Rom 11:29 (DR). The Greek for "without repentance" (*ametameletos*) literally means "unregretted." It is used only one other place in the New Testament (2 Cor 7:10). It is misleading to translate the word as "irrevocable" because that has given some people the erroneous impression that the Jews have an irrevocable covenant with God independent of Jesus Christ and the New Covenant.

334. This promise came through Abraham, not Moses (Gal 3:17–18). This means that the Covenant God gave through Abraham has been fulfilled in the New Covenant of Jesus Christ (Rom 4:16–17; Gal 3:29) and the "Old Covenant" God gave the Jews through Moses has been abolished by the same New Covenant of Christ (Rom 7:4; 2 Cor 3:14; Gal 3:10–12; Eph 2:15; Col 2:14; Heb 7:12, 18; 8:13; 10:9). As Paul says, in the New

Paul himself exercised authority to grant indulgences. In his First Letter to the Corinthians, Paul excommunicates a man who was having relations with his father's wife. (5:1). Paul excommunicates this man from the Church by declaring, "you are to deliver this man to Satan for the destruction of the flesh, that his spirit may be saved in the day of the Lord Jesus." (5:5). Many exegetes believe that Paul remits the punishment of excommunication in his Second Letter to the Corinthians. (2:1–11). After referring to the punishment of a certain member of the Church and the need to forgive him, Paul says, "And to whom you have pardoned any thing, I also. For, what I have pardoned, if I have pardoned any thing, for your sakes have I done it in the person of Christ."[335] In this verse, Paul grants an indulgence for the temporal punishment God imposed through Paul's binding authority, and does so "in the person of Christ."

How to Gain an Indulgence

To gain any indulgence, a person must first be Catholic. The Church's power to remit punishment through the keys is a jurisdictional power, and one must be subject to the Church's jurisdiction (that is, be a Catholic who is not excommunicated) in order to be subject to that power. The person must also be in a state of grace. Without grace, our penances have no merit in God's eyes and thus indulgences would avail us nothing. Moreover, a dead member of the body receives no inflow from the living members of the body, and one who is in mortal sin is spiritually dead. Further, the person must perform an act to which the pope has specifically ascribed

---

Covenant, "there is neither Jew nor Greek . . . for you are all one in Christ Jesus" (Gal 3:28).

335. 2 Cor 2:10 (DR).

an indulgence (as we mentioned, these acts are found in the Church's Enchiridion or handbook on indulgences).[336] Finally, the person must perform the indulgenced act with at least the habitual intention of gaining the indulgence.

To gain a plenary indulgence (complete remission of temporal punishment), the person must make a sacramental confession and receive the Eucharist. These sacraments do not have to be received on the day that the indulgenced work is performed, but should be received within a week before or after the work (but never more than twenty days before or after). The person must also pray for the intentions of the Sovereign Pontiff (the customary prayers are one Our Father, one Hail Mary, and one Glory Be). Finally, the person cannot have any attachment to sin , even venial sin. This means a person must not voluntarily retain any deliberate intention of permitting himself to commit venial sin. If any of these conditions are not met, the indulgence will be partial only. A person can gain only one plenary indulgence per day.[337] The extent to which a person's punishment is remitted depends both upon the person's degree of charity and the manner in which he performs the indulgenced work.

There are three principal ways to gain a partial indulgence

---

336. Even though granting indulgences is a power of jurisdiction and the grantor cannot exercise jurisdiction over himself, a prelate of the Church can benefit from those goods that are offered to the other members of the body (such as when he receives the Eucharist and distributes it to others). This means that the pope (and bishops) can gain the benefits of indulgences, even when he is the grantor. If not, the pope (and bishops) would be worse off since he could not make use of the treasury of merits he himself dispenses.

337. There is one exception to this rule: when a person, having already gained a plenary indulgence during the day, later finds himself in danger of death. Such a person can gain a second plenary indulgence connected with the Apostolic Blessing given during the Last Rites. A person can gain multiple partial indulgences per day.

(multiple partial indulgences can be gained throughout the day). First, the Church grants a partial indulgence to those who raise their mind to God in humble confidence while performing their daily tasks. One raises his mind to God by piously invoking, even mentally, the names of Jesus, Mary, and the saints, for example: "Jesus, have mercy on me"; "Heart of Jesus, I trust in Thee"; "Mary Immaculate"; "St. Joseph, pray for me." Whether one uses these or the many other traditional invocations (also called ejaculations), or whether one's prayer is individual or spontaneous, is not important. What is important is that it comes from the heart. How easy and beneficial is this practice, and yet how few people actually do it!

Secondly, the Church grants a partial indulgence to those who, motivated by charity, perform the spiritual and corporal works of mercy. As we have seen, the spiritual works include actions such as instructing the ignorant and comforting the afflicted. The corporal works include feeding the hungry and clothing the naked. Finally, the Church grants a partial indulgence to those who, in a spirit of penance, abstain from something permitted and pleasing to them. For example, a person who enjoys wine and is able to drink it (for example, he has no health problems, and it's not a day of fast) may choose to refrain from wine and drink water instead. We can think of countless other examples.

The Enchiridion also lists many prayers for which one may gain a partial indulgence. These prayers should be familiar to all Catholics, for example: Acts of faith, hope, charity, and contrition; the Guardian Angel prayer; the Angelus (the Regina Caeli during Easter); the Anima Christi; the Prayer Before a Crucifix; the Magnificat; the Memorare; the Hail Holy Queen (Salve Regina); the Tantum Ergo; the Come Holy Spirit; the Requiescant (Eternal rest grant unto them . . .); the many litanies (the Holy Name, Sacred Heart, Precious Blood, Mary, Joseph, the saints); the Sign of the Cross; and many others prayers and acts of piety. Indeed, Holy Mother Church has provided her children with many ways to lessen their punishments and increase their glory for heaven.

Certain indulgences are obtainable anytime and in almost any place, for example, reading Scripture continuously for a half hour or reciting five decades of the rosary in a church, family setting, or religious community. Plenary indulgences are granted for performing these pious practices, as well as for performing the Stations of the Cross or adoring the Blessed Sacrament for a half hour. Some indulgences are obtained on special days of the liturgical year, such as when certain prayers are recited, for example, on Holy Thursday, Good Friday, all Fridays during Lent, and All Souls' Day, to name a few. Other indulgences are obtainable on special occasions in one's life, such as First Communion, First Mass of newly-ordained priests, and the moment of death (*in articulo mortis*).[338]

Indulgences are also obtained through papal blessings, during diocesan synods and visits to the Patriarchal Basilicas in Rome. There are many other occasions for which the Church grants indulgences, reflecting the infinite mercy of God and His desire to free us from our debt of sin. Throughout the centuries, indulgences have inspired the faithful to good works and greater holiness. For more details, see Pope Paul VI's *Enchiridion on Indulgences* (1968).

The Blessed Virgin Mary has also revealed two promises

---

338. If a priest is not present to administer the last sacraments and the Apostolic Blessing, the Church still grants a plenary indulgence to the dying person if that person is properly disposed and has been in the habit of reciting some prayers during his lifetime.

for those who have been enrolled in the brown scapular.[339] First, the Mother of God appeared to Simon Stock as Our Lady of Mount Carmel on July 16, 1251 and gave him a scapular. She then said, "Whoever dies wearing this scapular shall not suffer eternal fire." Simon made the Blessed Mother's promise known throughout the Church, and Catholics have been wearing the brown scapular ever since. It is important to note that the Church does not attribute anything magical to the scapular or other sacramentals (the rosary, medals, holy water).[340] The Church teaches that attributing the efficacy of prayers or of sacramental signs to their mere external performance, apart from the interior dispositions that they demand, is to fall into superstition (CCC 2111). Superstition is a grave error that is completely opposed to the Catholic faith. Instead, sacramentals remind and inspire Catholics to live their faith externally as well as internally.

In another private revelation, the Mother of God revealed to Pope John XXII in 1322 what is called the Sabbatine (or Saturday) Privilege. Our Lady told him, "I, the Mother of Grace, shall descend on the Saturday after their death, and whomsoever I shall find in purgatory, I shall free." There are three conditions for obtaining this privilege. First, one must wear the brown scapular. Secondly, one must practice chastity according to his state in life. Thirdly, one must recite daily the Little Office of the Blessed Virgin Mary (but any priest with faculties can change this third requirement into another pious work, such as reciting a daily rosary or fasting twice a week). The Carmelite Order (a religious order

---

339. A scapular is a cloth string with two quadrilateral segments of woolen cloth (usually depicting Jesus and Mary), which is draped around the collar bones, hence the name "scapular."

340. A sacramental is a sacred sign which signifies the spiritual effects that are obtained through the graces of the Church (see CCC 1667–1673).

devoted to Our Lady of Mount Carmel) recommends that
the third requirement be not reduced to anything less than
the daily recitation of seven Our Fathers, seven Hail Marys
and seven Glory Be to the Fathers.

Final Thoughts

Although God does not want us to go to purgatory, His
strict justice and infinite holiness demand that we be freed
from sin and all its effects before entering eternal beatitude.
Not even the slightest hint of sin or its remnants can be in
the presence of our Thrice-holy God, who shows "no par-
tiality" to sinners.[341] Unfortunately, this truth gives many
people the impression that purgatory is unavoidable. Some
even pray that they simply "make it to purgatory." These
gloomy views are inconsistent with a Christ-centered life
that is wholly focused on gaining virtue and growing in holiness. The fact is, we can avoid purgatory altogether. Jesus
commanded us to "be perfect" in this life, and He doesn't
command the impossible. (Cf. Mt 5:48).

As we have seen, Holy Mother Church generously provides many ways to avoid purgatory and to assist those who
are suffering there. We have learned about the efficacy of
prayer, penances, the sacraments, and indulgences. We have
also learned about the value of patiently suffering the burdens of this life. Too many people are afraid to do penance,
and too few recognize the value of suffering. These works
not only make satisfaction for our sins but increase our grace
in this life and our glory in the next. Surely, offering these
works for the Holy Souls also redounds to our benefit, for
Christ says, "the measure you give will be the measure you

---

341. Cf. Lk 20:21; Acts 10:34; Rom 2:11; Gal 2:6; Eph 6:9; Col 3:25.

get, and still more will be given you." (Mk 4:24). Indeed, God will reward us in proportion to our generosity to the Holy Souls.

Ultimately, it comes down to removing in this life the causes of that which will detain us in the afterlife: sin. We can do this by living every day to do God's will and not our own. In short, we must love God with all our hearts and our neighbor as ourselves. With God's grace, we will not only be able to avoid mortal sin, but we will also be able to conquer habitual venial sins and sinful habits, which also blemish the soul.

Remember that God doesn't ask most people to be heroic. Rather, God asks us to do little things, like having patience with others and offering small acts of self-denial. This was the secret to sanctity for Therese of Lisieux, the Little Flower. Establishing a practice of small penances during this life will not only will diminish or eliminate our need for purgatory, but will also bring us great peace and joy.

I hope that this book will have awakened in you a holy fear of purgatory, and inspired you to live a holy life so you won't have to go there. Achieving such holiness in this life is difficult, but we can do it by the grace of God, which He offers us through Jesus Christ and the Catholic Church. As Paul says, "Now to him who by the power at work within us is able to do far more abundantly than all that we ask or think, to him be glory in the church and in Christ Jesus to all generations, for ever and ever. Amen." (Eph 3:20–21). May we be moved by God's grace so that we can attain more than we ever thought possible. I wish to close this book by giving the preacher Sirach (Ecclesiasticus) the final words:

> "In all you do, remember the end of your life,
> and then you will never sin." (Sir 7:36).

PRAYERS FOR THE SOULS IN PURGATORY[342]

A Prayer for the Souls in Purgatory

O MOST gentle Heart of Jesus, ever present in the Blessed Sacrament, ever consumed with burning love for the poor captive souls in purgatory, have mercy on the souls of Thy departed servants. Be not severe in Thy judgments, but let some drops of Thy Precious Blood fall upon the devouring flames. And do Thou, O merciful Savior, send Thy holy angels to conduct them to a place of refreshment, light, and peace. Amen.

A Prayer for the Dead

O GOD, the Creator and Redeemer of all the Faithful, grant unto the souls of Thy departed servants full remission of all their sins, that through the help of our pious supplications they may obtain that pardon which they have always desired, Thou Who lives and reigns world without end. Amen.

---

342. This selection of prayers used courtesy of TAN Books, an Imprint of Saint Benedict Press, LLC. Ecclesiastical Approbation 2002.

V. Eternal rest grant unto them, O Lord.
R. And let perpetual light shine upon them.
V. May they rest in peace. Amen.
R. And may the souls of all the faithful departed, through the mercy of God, rest in peace. Amen.

A Prayer for Our Dear Departed

O GOOD Jesus, Whose loving Heart was ever troubled by the sorrows of others, look with pity on the souls of our dear ones in Purgatory. O Thou Who didst "love Thine own," hear our cry for mercy, and grant that those whom Thou hast called from our homes and hearts may soon enjoy everlasting rest in the home of Thy love in heaven. Amen.
V. Eternal rest grant unto them, O Lord.
R. And let perpetual light shine upon them. Amen.

A Prayer for Deceased Parents

O GOD, who hast commanded us to honor our father and our mother, in Thy mercy have pity on the souls of my father and mother, and forgive them their trespasses, and make me to see them again in the joy of everlasting brightness. Through Christ Our Lord. Amen.

Offering of the Precious Blood

ETERNAL Father, I offer Thee the Precious Blood of Jesus Christ in satisfaction for my sins, in supplication for the Holy Souls in purgatory and for the needs of Holy Church. Amen.

A Prayer for the Poor Souls

MY JESUS, by the sorrows Thou didst suffer in Thine agony in the Garden, in Thy scourging and crowning with thorns, on the way to Calvary, and in Thy crucifixion and death, have mercy on the souls in purgatory, and especially on those that are most forsaken; do Thou deliver them from the dire torments they endure; call them and admit them to Thy most sweet embrace in Paradise. Amen.

Our Father . . . Hail Mary . . . Glory Be . . .

V. Eternal rest grant unto them, O Lord.
R. And let perpetual light shine upon them.
V. May the divine assistance remain always with us.
R. And may the souls of all the faithful departed, through the mercy of God, rest in peace. Amen.

Prayer for the Poor Souls, From the Roman Canon of the Mass

REMEMBER, O Lord, Thy servants and handmaids, N. and N., who have gone before us marked with the sign of faith and rest in the sleep of peace. To these, O Lord, and to all who rest in Christ, grant, we beseech Thee, a place of comfort, light and peace. Through the same Christ our Lord. Amen.

A Prayer for a Deceased Priest

O GOD, Thou didst raise Thy servant, N., to the sacred priesthood of Jesus Christ, according to the Order of Melchisedech, giving him the sublime power to offer the Eternal Sacrifice, to bring the Body and Blood of Thy Son

Jesus Christ down upon the altar, and to absolve the sins of men in Thine own holy name. We beseech Thee to reward his faithfulness and to forget his faults, admitting him speedily into Thy holy presence, there to enjoy forever the recompense of his labors. This we ask through Jesus Christ Thy Son our Lord. Amen.

A Prayer Addressed to the Poor Souls in Purgatory

O HOLY souls in purgatory, thou art the certain heirs of Heaven. Thou art most dear to Jesus, as the trophies of His Precious Blood, and to Mary, Mother of Mercy. Obtain for me, through thine intercession, the grace to lead a holy life, to die a happy death, and to attain to the blessedness of eternity in Heaven.

Dear suffering souls, who long to be delivered in order to praise and glorify God in Heaven, by thine unfailing pity, help me in the needs which distress me at this time, particularly (here mention your request), so that I may obtain relief and assistance from God.

In gratitude for this intercession, I offer to God on thy behalf the satisfactory merits of my prayers, works, joys, and sufferings of this day (week, month, or whatever space of time you wish to designate). Amen.

A Prayer for and to the Holy Souls in Purgatory

O MOST compassionate Jesus, have mercy on the souls detained in purgatory, for whose redemption Thou didst take upon Thyself our nature and endure a bitter death. Mercifully hear their sighs, look with pity upon the tears that they now shed before Thee, and by virtue of Thy Passion, release them from the pains due to their sins. O most merciful Jesus, let Thy Precious Blood reach down into Purgatory and refresh and revive the captive souls who suffer there. Stretch out to them Thy strong right hand, and bring them forth into the place of refreshment, light and peace. Amen.

O blessed souls! We have prayed for thee! We entreat thee, who art so dear to God, and who art certain of never losing Him, to pray for us poor miserable sinners who are in danger of being damned and of losing God forever. Amen.

For Our Deceased Servicemen

THOU art all powerful, O God, and livest forever in light and joy. Look with pity and love, we beseech Thee, upon those men who have bravely fought and gallantly died for our country. By laying down their lives, they have showed supreme love for others. We implore Thee to accept their sacrifice and their belief in the justice of the cause for which they died. May their offering not be in vain. Deign to forgive any sins or misdeeds they may have committed. Bring them quickly, we implore Thee, into Thine august presence, where fear, sadness, mourning, and death no longer exist. Have pity, in Thy loving kindness, on those they leave behind. In Thine own inscrutable ways, make good their absence, and lavishly bestow Thy love and consolations upon those deprived of their presence. This we ask of Thee in the name of Jesus Christ, our King. Amen.

Eternal Rest

V. Eternal rest grant unto them, O Lord.
R. And let perpetual light shine upon them.
V. May their souls, and the souls of all the faithful departed, through the mercy of God, rest in peace.
R. Amen.

A Novena for the Poor Souls

Sunday

O LORD God Almighty, I beseech Thee by the Precious Blood which Thy divine Son Jesus shed in the Garden, deliver the souls in purgatory, and especially that one which is the most forsaken of all, and bring it into Thy glory, where it may praise and bless Thee forever. Amen.

Our Father . . . Hail Mary . . . Glory Be . . . Eternal rest . . .

Monday

O LORD God Almighty, I beseech Thee by the Precious Blood which Thy divine Son Jesus shed in His cruel scourging, deliver the souls in purgatory, and among them all, especially that soul which is nearest to its entrance into Thy glory, that it may soon begin to praise Thee and bless Thee forever. Amen.

Our Father . . . Hail Mary . . . Glory Be . . . Eternal rest . . .

Tuesday

O LORD God Almighty, I beseech Thee by the Precious Blood of Thy divine Son Jesus that was shed in His bitter crowning with thorns, deliver the souls in purgatory, and among them all, particularly that soul which is in the greatest need of our prayers, in order that it may not long be delayed in praising Thee in Thy glory and blessing Thee forever. Amen.

Our Father ... Hail Mary ... Glory Be ... Eternal rest ...

Wednesday

O LORD God Almighty, I beseech Thee by the Precious Blood of Thy divine Son Jesus that was shed in the streets of Jerusalem, whilst He carried on His sacred shoulders the heavy burden of the Cross, deliver the souls in purgatory, and especially that one which is richest in merits in Thy sight, so that, having soon attained the high place in glory to which it is destined, it may praise Thee triumphantly and bless Thee forever. Amen.

Our Father ... Hail Mary ... Glory Be ... Eternal rest ...

Thursday

O LORD God Almighty, I beseech Thee by the Precious Blood of Thy divine Son Jesus which He Himself, on the night before His Passion, gave as meat and drink to His beloved apostles and bequeathed to His holy Church to be the perpetual sacrifice and life-giving nourishment of His faithful people, deliver the souls in purgatory, but most of all, that soul which was most devoted to this Mystery of infinite love, in order that it may praise Thee therefore, together with Thy divine Son and the Holy Spirit in Thy glory forever. Amen.

Our Father . . . Hail Mary . . . Glory Be . . . Eternal rest . . .

Friday

O LORD God Almighty, I beseech Thee by the Precious Blood which Jesus Thy divine Son did shed this day upon the tree of the Cross, especially from His sacred hands and feet, deliver the souls in purgatory, and particularly that soul for whom I am most bound to pray, in order that I may not be the cause which hinders Thee from admitting it quickly to the possession of Thy glory, where it may praise Thee and bless Thee for evermore. Amen.

Our Father . . . Hail Mary . . . Glory Be . . . Eternal rest . . .

Saturday

O LORD God Almighty, I beseech Thee by the Precious Blood which gushed forth from the sacred side of Thy divine Son Jesus in the presence of and to the great sorrow of His most holy Mother, deliver the souls in purgatory, and among them all, especially that soul which has been most devout to this noble Lady, that it may come quickly into Thy glory, there to praise Thee in her, and her in Thee, through all ages. Amen.

Our Father . . . Hail Mary . . . Glory Be . . . Eternal rest . . .

On Every Day of the Novena

V. O Lord, hear my prayer.

R. And let my cry come unto Thee.

O GOD, the Creator and Redeemer of all the faithful, grant unto the souls of Thy servants and handmaids the remission of all their sins, that through our devout supplications, they may obtain the pardon they have always desired, Who lives and reigns world without end. Amen.

Eternal rest . . .

Prayer of St. Gertrude the Great

O ETERNAL Father, I offer Thee the Most Precious Blood of Thy Divine Son, Jesus, in union with the Masses said throughout the world today, for all the holy souls in Purgatory, and for sinners everywhere—for sinners in the Universal Church, for those in my own home, and for those within my family. Amen.

Prayer for the Dying

O MOST Merciful Jesus, lover of souls, I pray Thee, by the agony of Thy most Sacred Heart, and by the sorrows of Thine Immaculate Mother, to wash in Thy Most Precious Blood the sinners of the whole world who are now in their agony and who will die today.

Heart of Jesus, once in agony, have mercy on the dying! Amen.

O Mother most merciful,
pray for the souls in Purgatory!

ABOUT THE AUTHOR

JOHN SALZA is a well-noted Catholic apologist, author, and speaker. He is the creator of ScriptureCatholic.com, one of the most popular apologetics sites on the Internet. ScriptureCatholic.com is a veritable library of over 2,000 Scripture citations and over 800 quotes from the early Church Fathers that explain and defend the Catholic faith. The site also includes a popular Q&A section and other helpful resources.

John is a frequent guest and host on Catholic radio including Searching the Word and The Drew Mariani Show. John has his own apologetics feature on Relevant Radio called "Relevant Answers" which runs six times a day, seven days a week. John also has a daily apologetics spot on the Eternal Word Television Network's (EWTN) Global Catholic radio program called "Catholic Q&A." John has appeared numerous times on EWTN to discuss a variety of apologetics topics.

John is the author of *Why Catholics Cannot Be Masons* (TAN Books), as well as the following books by Our Sunday Visitor: *The Biblical Basis for the Catholic Faith; The Biblical Basis for the Papacy; The Biblical Basis for the Eucharist; The Biblical Basis for Tradition;* and, *Masonry Unmasked: An Insider Reveals the Secrets of the Lodge*. John is also the author of the booklet "Honor Your Mother, Defend Your Queen: A Marian Treasury" (Relevant Radio).